"As Western culture abandons [its] Christian roots, it is becoming [essential to think] carefully about how to respond. [...] theological reasons for learning such skills and practical guidance for getting there."

**D. A. CARSON,** President, The Gospel Coalition; Research Professor of New Testament, Trinity Evangelical Divinity School

"A clear and practical challenge to engage in sharing the gospel in our culture. Inspiring and biblical. Buy *Plugged In* today and apply the truth in these pages to your everyday context."

**GAVIN CALVER,** Director of Mission, Evangelical Alliance; Chair of Spring Harvest

"Without sacrificing depth or nuance, Daniel Strange makes cultural engagement accessible to the layman. *Plugged In* is a fun read, traversing diverse cultural landscapes. And what's more, he shows how each of these carries its own theological challenge, and how we can respond as Christians in ways that are winsome and gracious, rather than crusty and insular."

**TED TURNAU,** Author, *Popologetics*

"Whatever your take on the relationship between Christianity and culture, I encourage you to hear Dan's brilliant contribution to this important discussion."

**KRISH KANDIAH,** Founding Director, Home for Good

"This book is both thought-provoking and practical. Daniel Strange skilfully guides the reader on a journey to both confront and connect with what they see around them in the media, film and television. A much-needed book!"

**NOLA LEACH,** Chief Executive, CARE

"A compelling, biblically rich and decidedly practical guide to engaging Christianly with culture. I'm excited about putting it into the hands or onto the tablets of the rising generations."

**MEL LACY,** Director, Growing Young Disciples

"In this gem of a book, seasoned author Daniel Strange manages what few people could do. He pre-digests the unwieldy and complex realm of culture studies and makes it unaffectedly clear. Most of all he tells us why we should care about engaging culture, and he makes crucial suggestions for how to do that. All of it is in a writing style that is full of imagination, enviably lucid, down-home without being folksy. This will be the go-to text for years, even decades, to come."

**WILLIAM EDGAR,** Professor of Apologetics, Westminster Theological Seminary, Philadelphia

"It's vital we think about how being a Christian shapes the way we interact with the culture around us, and I know of no better guide than *Plugged In*. Dan Strange provides both a biblical framework and practical nuts-and-bolts tools, and shows how culture can be a great starting point for speaking of Christ with our friends and colleagues. I warmly commend it."

**TIM CHESTER,** Faculty member, Crosslands Training; Author, *Enjoying God*

"A fresh, generous and humorous look at how we can engage with culture intentionally, enjoyably and effectively. Years of reflecting and teaching on this topic have enabled Dan Strange to distil his best insights down to this small but deceptively sharp and persuasive book. The modern church needs tools like this. I recommend it wholeheartedly."

**RICHARD CUNNINGHAM,** Director, UCCF: the Christian Unions

"Dan Strange helps us to 'stop and think': to consider all that we see and hear and do through the lens of Scripture. This book is designed to equip this generation of Christ's people to engage faithfully with the culture around us for God's glory."

**SHARON JAMES,** The Christian Institute

Daniel Strange

# PLUGGED IN

*Dedicated to Bill (Edgar) and Ted (Turnau)*
*for being both mentors and friends*
*on this excellent adventure.*

Plugged In

*Connecting your faith with what you watch, read, and play*

© Daniel Strange 2019.

Reprinted 2019 (twice), 2020.

Published by:
The Good Book Company

thegoodbook.com | www.thegoodbook.co.uk
thegoodbook.com.au | thegoodbook.co.nz | thegoodbook.co.in

Unless indicated, all Scripture references are taken from the Holy Bible, New International Version. Copyright © 2011 Biblica, Inc.TM Used by permission.

ISBN: 9781909919419 | Printed in the UK

Design by André Parker

# CONTENTS

# FOREWORD

## BY TIMOTHY KELLER

I once heard one of my professors tell a story about Paul Tillich, a German theologian who was very prominent in academic circles. When my professor was a young faculty member at a seminary in the United States, he was given the task of moderating the discussion after a public lecture by Tillich. Students began asking questions, but each time, the guest lecturer completely reformulated and "corrected" the question before answering it.

Finally my professor summoned some courage and said, "Professor Tillich, that wasn't really the student's question. Could you answer the question the student actually asked?" The response was quick and withering: "No, because they aren't asking the right questions." Maybe that was partly true, my professor concluded, but the result of this tactic was that the students completely tuned out and dismissed Tillich.

Dan Strange knows that contemporary Christians are a lot like that ineffective lecturer. We believe "Jesus is the answer," but we are so deaf to the cultural forces around us that we often present him as answering questions that people are not asking. Of course, because of sin, human beings do fail to ask the most fundamental question of all: "How can I, a sinner, be made right with a holy and just God?" And yet, as Dan shows in this book, the image of God in all people and common grace mean that people also ask some right questions: "Who am I? What is meaning in life? How can I find true joy and fulfillment?"

Every culture produces "texts"—things to watch, read, and play—that are based on answers to those big questions. Dan Strange shows us, in the most accessible way I've ever seen, how to do Christian cultural analysis. That is, he shows us how to identify the culture's particular answers to those big questions in any text. Then he demonstrates how to both critique those answers and yet affirm the basic aspirations, and finally how to redirect people toward Christ as the true fulfillment of their quests and the true answer to their questions.

The basic method used here is one formulated by some 20th-century missiologists. The name "subversive fulfillment" perfectly describes the approach. Christians are to show members of other religions and world-views that the gospel fulfills basic human longings and aspirations, but at the same time they are to critique the false idols in every culture that people look to for the satisfaction of those longings. Subversive fulfillment avoids the twin errors of syncretism and irrelevance. Sin must not just be denounced in general, but in the particular idolatrous forms found in the culture.

Salvation must not just be declared in general, but as fulfilling the very hopes that the culture wrongly puts in its idols.

In *Plugged In*, Dan Strange takes this method, brings it into the 21st century, and makes it wonderfully useable for any reader. Dan convincingly shows that this is the way Paul preached. But the approach is not merely a strategy for evangelistic conversations (though it certainly is that). Dan shows that it is also a way for Christians to understand the world they live in and the cultural texts that are coming at them every day, so that they can live faithfully "in the world but not of it."

Even more, Dan is calling for subversive fulfillment to pervade our approach to all our communicating—in public preaching and teaching, personal shepherding, instructing, and conversing. It means never simply beating on people from the outside, saying, "I am right and you are completely wrong." Nor is it merely a way to show how up-to-date and relevant Christianity is. It involves both respecting and contradicting. It means challenging people, but showing them that their efforts fail on their own terms. And it means offering them, on gospel terms, what all human hearts rightly need—a meaning that suffering can't take away; a satisfaction not based on circumstances; a freedom that doesn't destroy love and community; an identity that doesn't elude you, crush you, or lead you to exclude others; a basis for justice that doesn't turn you into a new oppressor; a relief from shame and guilt without resorting to relativism; and a hope that can enable you to face anything with poise, even death.

There are now plenty of books calling us to find new ways of connecting our gospel presentation to the needs and questions of people in a secular, pluralistic society. And there are plenty of other books calling for us to live faithfully in a post-Christian Western culture, neither simply withdrawing nor assimilating into it. But Dan's book *Plugged In* actually tells and shows us how to do it. There really is nothing else like the book now in your hands.

# INTRODUCTION

We live in a world of constant information.

Just think about your day so far. Here's how my morning looked...

Alarm turns on the radio: government minister being grilled over education policy.

Walk the dog, headphones firmly in, listening to a film-review podcast.

Make the kids packed lunches with radio in background, trying to stop our youngest from activating Alexa and playing the Power Rangers theme tune at ear-bleeding levels. (Tell me: Why is it, when I shout, "Alexa, stop", she doesn't, but when my kids tell her to stop, she immediately does?)

Scan the news app: politics, economy, sport, economy, politics.

Check the weather app: rain.

I've only been awake for forty-five minutes and already my senses have been subjected to a barrage of information.

Technology experts have stated that the amount of recorded information generated from the dawn of humanity to 2003 was in the order of 5 exabytes of data, where an exabyte indicates 1000000000000000000 bytes. From 2003 to 2010, we generated an additional 5 exabytes. By 2018, 90% of the world's data had been generated in the previous two years alone. When you consider that 400 hours of new video is uploaded to YouTube every minute, it's hardly surprising. That's a lot of prank videos to get through.

## TELLING STORIES

But people don't take on information as bytes. Our smartphones might be downloading bytes of information, but our brains aren't—the unit our minds and hearts operate in is stories. Now when I say "stories", I don't mean the sort of stories you were taught to write in school, with a beginning, a middle and an end (usually a very predictable one). These stories are all the experiences, feelings, imagination and ideas that we communicate from one human being to another. We read them in the newspaper, we watch them in the cinema, we hear them sung from the car stereo, we glance at them on Instagram, we frame them in our homes.

All of us spend a lot of our waking moments taking in, and telling, these cultural stories. Recent research showed that the average American consumes over ten hours of media every day. It's thought that you'll spend seven and a half years of your life watching TV, and over five years on social media. But there are so many hours in a day, right? No wonder that it's been said of the TV-streaming service Netflix that their greatest competition isn't another company but the human need for sleep.

Yet many of us find this barrage of information overwhelming, at least some of the time. We feel like the title of the old 1940's Rodgers and Hart song: "Bewitched, bothered and bewildered". Search engines have given us access to more information than the *Encyclopedia Britannica* ever could (if you're too young to know what this is—google it!), but we are never sure that we have the right answer.

All this information presents us with a problem: how do we know what's true? So we look for an authority we can rely on. By and large, most people still seem to have a deep-seated desire to trust people and institutions. We want our athletes to be dope free and our sports administrators not to succumb to a bribe. Some of us nostalgically remember when kids could play on the street, and when we could go and buy milk from the corner shop without locking the front door. But now we can't read a news story online without wondering whether it's a fake. It seems that our social-media diets are dictated either by clever algorithms or sinister corporations.

For Christians, there's an added question: how do we know what's *right*? As followers of Jesus, we want to think, speak and act in a way that honours him. We want to "set [our] minds on things above" (Colossians 3 v 2), but in reality, most of the time our minds are submerged in a constant stream of stories. The problem is not that these cultural stories are bad in and of themselves; it's more that we're ill-equipped to know quite what to make of them. How does what I watch on a Saturday night link with what I hear at church on a Sunday morning? We barely begin to think about it before the next thing starts on autoplay. So more often, we just don't.

I'm no different, and I think about this kind of stuff for a living. Moral ambiguity abounds. A while ago I read an interview with Miley Cyrus, the Disney-star turned global pop icon. On the one hand I read, "I am literally open to every single thing that is consenting and doesn't involve an animal and everyone is of age. Everything that's legal, I'm down with. Yo, I'm down with any adult—anyone over the age of 18 who is down to love me. I don't relate to being boy or girl, and I don't have to have my partner relate to boy or girl." However, towards the end of interview she started describing her homeless charity: "I can't drive by in my [expletive] Porsche and not [expletive] do something. I see it all day: people in their Bentleys and their Rolls and their Ubers, driving past these [veterans] who have fought for our country, or these young women who have been raped. I was doing a show two nights ago ... dressed like a butterfly. How is that fair? How am I so lucky?"[1]

What's my reaction? How do I reconcile Miley's sexual philosophy with her sense of social justice? Do I laugh? Do I cry? Do I rage? Do I just sit in stunned silence? Do I do all the above? Or maybe all I can do is emoji: 😫

Using old-fashioned words, a recent poem by Anthony Thwaite seems to express how many of us feel. He describes the poem as "a weary sigh by an old man".

Oh dear
How many times these days I say those words,
Muttering them quietly under my breath
Or petulantly as the telephone rings
Or shocked at some reported piece of news
Or simply as a constant formula
For things that pass by daily, and are gone
Into the nowhere that life seems to be
Day after day, as if unceasingly.
Too soft to be an expletive, too repetitive
To have distinction, more sigh than cry of rage,
How many times these days I say those words
And may well say them till the day I die
When everything's worn out and stiff with age
And I have nothing else to say but 'Why?'[2]

In short, when we look around, we might have a "Keep calm and carry on" poster on our wall, but we're not particularly calm and we are finding it increasingly difficult to carry on.

### THREE REACTIONS

If you've been a Christian for a while, then chances are that you've heard the old cliché that we need to be "in the world but not of the world". But what does that even mean? Or perhaps you've read the bit where Peter tells us to "always be prepared to give an answer to everyone who asks you to give the reason for the hope that you have" (1 Peter 3 v 15), but you're scared that someone might actually ask you, because you wouldn't know what to say. What if it was someone like Miley?

So what do we do? I think many Christians respond to culture in one of three ways (and the rest of us respond in a mixture of all three).

Some of us just want to *"look in"*. We stick our heads in the sand, get into our holy huddle and Christian bubble, and hang on for dear life. We put our fingers in our ears so that we can't hear the noise outside, while at the same time singing loudly to one another about Jesus coming back soon when all the outside stuff will go away. Until then, we keep ourselves safe from worldly influences by only ever reading Amish romance novels or the latest releases from our favourite celebrity pastor. If we were in therapy, this would be called our sanctified "flight" response.

Some of us instinctively *"lash out"*. This is our sanctified "fight" response. We get all huffy, red-faced and finger-pointy at the culture around us. Or we just tut and roll our eyes at sex scenes in films or the bad language on TV. At its worst, our healthy belief in judgment turns into an ugly judgmentalism. Our proclamation of the good news of Jesus is heard as a rant on morality. And then we wonder why people "out there" don't want to come and be with us "in here".

Then, some of us end up *"looking like"*. Whatever the motivation, our lives—and our cultural diets—are indistinguishable from the neighbour's next door, and our churches end up looking not much different from the local sports club. Maybe it's a well-intentioned drive to be "relevant". Maybe it's a reaction against judgmentalism. Maybe it's simply an indulgence of our sinful nature. Whatever it is, we struggle to be recognised as "a chosen people, a royal priesthood, a holy nation, God's special possession" (1 Peter 2 v 9). We have become experts at conforming "to the pattern of this world" when we've expressly been told not to (Romans 12 v 2).

Look in, lash out, look like: which response are you most prone to?

## ENGAGE

Let me suggest that there is another way—and that's what this book is all about. Because it is possible to be truly "in" the world instead of "looking in"—without being "of" the world and looking like it.

It's possible to engage with culture in a way that's truthful and gracious, not angry and self-righteous.

It's possible to consume culture without either being bewitched by it—buying into everything it tells us—or bewildered by it.

It's possible to watch TV and read novels and play video games in a way that actually feeds our faith rather than withers it.

It's even possible for you—yes, you—to be that person who starts off talking to a friend about last night's football and ends up talking about Jesus.

And that's what this book will equip you to do. It will help you to process the cultural stories you hear every day. I want to give you the confidence to think about and speak about culture in a way that points people to a bigger and better reality: the story of King Jesus and his cosmic plan for this world. Because you can't escape culture. But you can engage culture.

# 1. WHAT CULTURE IS (AND WHY YOU SHOULD CARE)

**A**s you might have guessed from the front cover, this is a book about engaging with culture. But what is "culture", exactly? It's a notoriously difficult term to define and has a complicated history.

If you're into etymology (the study of words and where they come from), it's helpful to know that the original word "culture" has three senses coming from its Latin roots. *Colere*, referring to agriculture. That's about tilling the ground and growing things. *Colonus*, which is to do with the idea of inhabiting something. And finally *cultus*, which is to do with honour and worship. Store these away for now because we'll come back to them later.

Today, we use the term "culture" in different ways, mainly as a reflection of the way it's been passed around between various academic disciplines.

## THE "ARTS" DEFINITION
Coming from the arts and literature, "culture" is still associated with the idea of refined taste and manners.

It's about *being* "cultured". So Rupert (a.k.a. "Rups"), who goes punting in Oxford with a picnic and Pimms, reading P. G. Wodehouse out loud to his friends, before going to play cricket and then spend a night at the opera, is being cultured. Garry (a.k.a "Gaz") going for a kick around in the park and then down Southend seafront to cruise in his Ford Escort and pick up a kebab and girl from Tots nightclub is *not* being cultured: he's uncouth! By this definition, culture has a definite sense of "oughtness": there are things that belong to culture, and other things that definitely do not.

Of course, if you're reading this and you're not British, then those descriptions of Rups and Gaz might have made little sense to you, because you're from a different... well, *culture*. Which takes us on to our next definition...

## THE "SOCIAL SCIENCES" DEFINITION

Then the social sciences took ownership. Here, the definition of "culture" is less elitist and broader in its scope. All human beings *belong* to a culture, and every culture brings its own distinctive contribution. Moreover, culture doesn't refer to just one part of our existence, such as the arts. Instead it refers to every activity and artefact that humans create—both individually and as communities and societies—which gives them order, identity and meaning. It's everything from music and stories to what you eat and what you wear (and when); from what happens at a wedding to whether it's socially acceptable to whistle in the street or not. It covers the ordinary and the everyday.

While not as elitist as the "arts" definition of culture, in this "social sciences" view, it was, and still is, possible to claim that some cultures have more to contribute to human existence than others. Distinctions might be made between "primitive" or "advanced" cultures, or between "high" culture and "pop" culture. Of course, such distinctions are up for debate and can be controversial.

For example, measure your reaction in our current cultural setting to this comment of General Charles James Napier in the 1850s. As Commander-in-Chief of the British forces in colonial India, he said the following when Hindu priests complained to him about the ban on *sati*, the practice of burning widows alive on their husband's funeral pyres:

> Be it so. This burning of widows is your custom:
> prepare the funeral pile. But my nation has also
> a custom. When men burn women alive, we
> hang them, and confiscate all their property. My
> carpenters shall therefore erect gibbets on which to
> hang all concerned, when the widow is consumed.
> Let us all act according to national customs.[3]

It's safe to say that no Foreign Office spokesperson would say that today. Our reactions to General Napier demonstrate changes in cultural sensibilities in the intervening 160 years. We appear to be far more reluctant today to make *prescriptions* about cultural practices—that is, judging whether something is right or wrong. Instead we prefer to stick to *descriptions* of cultural practices, which carry no value judgements. This is the social-science way of doing things. However, this alleged neutrality does grate with our daily experience and natural instincts. We say we "don't want to judge" and "each to their own", but deep down we don't find it easy to separate facts and values. Something within us wants to give our opinion on *sati* (or give our opinion on Napier's opinion on *sati*!).

## THE "CULTURAL STUDIES" DEFINITION

In the last 50 years, "cultural studies" has become an academic discipline all to itself. It's a pretty complex area which draws on all kinds of other fields of study, most noticeably semiotics: the study of signs and symbols and how we interpret them. Cultural studies is interested in the subjects of power and politics, and how these relate to ethnicity, class, age and gender.

Part of what makes it complicated is the recognition that cultures are not static, fixed and separated "things" but are fluid, evolving and interconnected. It's confusing and messy because the world is confusing and messy. Culture and cultural studies are about identity—how it's defined and, more importantly, by whom. And cultural theorists use all kinds of complicated terms that you may never have heard of unless you play Scrabble. Annoyingly though, they do seem to describe our world and our state of mind.

It's all about our "glocal" world: recognising both global and local influences. It's all about "hybridity": recognising that we seem to be made up of a mix of cultural identities. It's all about "liminality": the disorientation of living in the midst of cultural change—in the gap "in between" where we've been and where we are going.

So, it's McDonald's looking like McDonald's the world over, but selling beer in some countries and not others. It's how we have food halls with lots of international cuisine, but with the hard edges taken off for mass consumption. It's rap and hip-hop that originated "straight outta Compton" but that have gone worldwide and have inspired British rap, French rap and more. It's making the old new again. It's *Star Wars: The Force Awakens*. It's lo-fi music and the resurgence of vinyl records. It's going retro—my kids wanting to wear sweatshirts that I wore in the '80s. But the strange thing is that the more identities we seem to collect, the less we are sure about who we are.

## THE "STORIES" DEFINITION

We see elements of truth in all three of these definitions. But as we come to see what the Bible says about culture over the next few chapters, I want to suggest a more helpful way of framing our thinking. Rather than seeing culture as a "thing", we'll be thinking of culture as the way we live in the world and interpret what's around us. For the purposes of this book, we'll define culture like this:

Culture is the stories we tell that express meaning about the world.

Two things to note here.

First, culture expresses meaning. It's the way we make meaning and sense of the world, even if our conclusion is that there is no meaning. Culture is the way we communicate and "live" our worldview—what's important, what's right and wrong, what is true and how we can know it, and how to be happy. And this is where the definitions start to get confusing, because when a group of people share the same worldview, we tend to call this "a culture" too (as in British culture or Japanese culture). This "worldview-culture" is primarily expressed through the cultural stories we tell, and the stories we listen to in turn slowly shape our worldview.

For example, some cultures have roots that prize the individual over the community and vice versa. Or what about this? In the UK, most of us expect a government-run health service which meets the needs of everyone, is free at the point of delivery, and is based on clinical need, not ability to pay—the celebrations for the National Health Service's 70th anniversary both reflect and reinforce it's position as a national treasure. Yet this is certainly not a description of other cultures' health-care provision, nor is it universally believed to be something that should be aspired to!

Second, culture is stories. Some stories use words; others are wordless. Some stories are fictional; others are factual. Some stories are long; others are 140 characters.

So your favourite soap opera has a plot with characters who fall out, make up and get together. But that story expresses meaning about the world—the plot communicates something about what the people making it think is heroic, what is despicable, and what is truly valuable. As do *Trainspotting* and *Titanic*, "Sweet Child O'

Mine" and "Single Ladies", *Pride and Prejudice* and *Real Housewives of Orange County*, Facebook Messenger and Mario Kart, Tracy Emin's *My Bed* and da Vinci's *Mona Lisa*, Buzzfeed and BBC News. All of these—in one way or another—are telling stories that express meaning about the world around us.

We'll explore this definition in the context of the Bible's storyline in the next two chapters, but before that, let's stand back to consider another question: why should Christians bother engaging with culture?

## FOUR REASONS WHY YOU SHOULD CARE ABOUT CULTURE

Of course, given that you've picked up this book and read this far, it's clear that you do already care about culture to some extent. But just in case you need convincing, let me lay out four reasons why, as Christians, we should be seeking to engage with it—instead of looking in, lashing out or looking like it.

We'll pick up many of these themes in later chapters, but consider this a fast-paced overview of where we're heading and why.

### 1. We care because we've got no choice

Let's get straight down to it: we have no choice but to engage with culture. Whether we like it or not, engaging with culture is inevitable because created humans are cultural beings. You both consume and create culture every day. You can't help it. But you also *belong* to a culture—and that's an undeniable part of who you are.

As Christians, our identity is first and foremost as people who are "in Christ". But this spiritual reality doesn't cancel out the earthly reality that we all come from somewhere. We were all born at a certain time and in a certain place, into a certain family. We all have our own identity that we express in the stories we create, and a set of cultural stories that we grew up with that have in turn formed our identity.

I am a 40-something, 15-stone/210lbs, 6-foot-2-inches, ethnically half white/half Indo-Guyanese British man, born in Southend-on-Sea in Essex, converted through a youth organisation called the Boys Brigade. I'm married with a load of kids, and I teach in a theological college, watch West Ham United Football Club and am a jazz and classical music geek. All this makes a difference to how I hear other people and how I am heard by other people, even though I'm first and foremost "in Christ".

And it makes a difference to how I read the Bible, how I communicate the gospel, and what I do when I gather with other Christians as a church. For example, at my church we meet on a Sunday morning, I sit on a chair next to my wife, and I keep my shoes on for the duration of the service. But if my church was in Lahore instead of London, things would be very different! Or think about the example I gave earlier about health-care provision. Can you imagine what different issues might arise and what decisions might have to be made by a local church and its leadership in a country where there is state health-care provision compared with one where there isn't?

None of us can escape our culture when we approach the Bible—all of us look at it through a particular cultural filter, like coloured lenses in a pair of glasses. As one of my Christian heroes, the Dutch theologian J. H. Bavinck, has said:

Each time the gospel is preached in a different language, to a different people, it has to transmute [translate] a variety of words, as it were, and give them new content. The gospel does not find anywhere in the world a ready language that fits completely and absolutely like a garment.[4]

The gospel doesn't "fit" one particular culture—it's bigger than that. But I, of course, have the tendency to assume that the perfect gospel "fit" is English and middle-class; that the way we do things as Christians together is the way it should be and always has been. Or I assume that I'm above culture and unaffected by my context. This lack of cultural self-awareness can and does lead me into trouble, especially when it comes to working with and worshipping alongside Christians from other backgrounds. If I don't think carefully about culture, I can't discern when I have confused gospel and culture, and become either too rigid or too flexible.

Please don't mishear me. The gospel is not so culturally fluid that it ceases to have any meaning at all. God reveals himself truthfully and clearly. He is not located in and limited by culture. He is the unique Creator and distinct from everything else which is created. So although no human can *communicate* gospel truth in a way that is unaffected by culture, that *truth* itself *can be* above and beyond culture.

We can't escape our culture, so we need to be aware of it. But there's more to it than that: we can and should *embrace* it, because we recognise and celebrate the wonderful combination of *both* Christian cultural unity, which is not a bland uniformity, and Christian cultural diversity, which is not ugly division.

Our monthly bring-and-share church lunches in East Finchley are an amazing, dizzying mix of dishes from all over the world that reflect the nationalities in our congregation: West Indian, Nigerian, Malaysian, Indonesian, Iranian and British just to name a few. We might dress a little differently on a Sunday. English might not be the first language spoken, so some things might be lost in translation. Our musical tastes might be very different. But because we're brothers and sisters in Christ, we can still worship our Saviour side by side—and that's beautiful. Indeed, as a pastor friend of mine says, in this way the church is meant to be a "show-house" of the new heaven and new earth.

## 2. We care about following Jesus

Second, we engage with culture because we want to follow Jesus faithfully as we live in his world. And part of living in his world involves consuming culture and creating culture. Let's take both of these in turn.

First, we want to be faithful to Jesus as we consume culture. When the apostle John wrote his first letter to Christians in Asia, the final thing he wanted his audience to hear as it was read aloud was this: "Dear children, keep yourselves from idols" (1 John 5 v 21). We'll have more to say about idolatry as we go on, but for now, let's define idols as counterfeit god-substitutes which have captured our hearts, when our hearts should be captured by Jesus. In order to keep ourselves from idols, we need to be able to recognise them and learn how they operate. This is easier said than done. I think we are often like the guy who, upon seeing the sign "Beware, pickpockets operate in this area", determinedly puts his wallet in his back pocket because he's sure he'd feel any attempted pinch from there. After all, he's got a sensitive bum. You know how that story ends...

Like pickpockets, idols are hard to spot. Idolatry is subtle because Satan is crafty and cunning. Idols don't approach us with "I'm an idol: keep yourself from me" tattooed on their foreheads. No, idols are *counterfeit* god-substitutes—and the better the counterfeit, the harder they are to identify. Most of us know to look out for well-known idols to do with money and sex. And in our churches we're getting better at talking about "deep idols", such as power, comfort, approval and control. But I think that when it comes to *cultural* idols, we're pretty insensitive, partly because of what I've already said above: we either think culture doesn't really matter or we think we aren't cultural beings. The problem is that culture is comprehensive: there is no escape.

So how are you doing at keeping yourself from idols in your voting? In your decision about where the kids go to school? About your choice of this evening's television?

About all you do in all the hours of your life that isn't "church stuff"?

There's more though. What I've said so far could sound passive, defensive and reactive. We also need to recognise that as human beings, we are designed to be culture creators and builders. Keeping ourselves from idols requires us to put something else in their place, because our hearts are hardwired to worship *something*. More on this in the next chapter.

### 3. We care about telling others about Jesus

We engage with culture because we care about evangelism and apologetics. Now, it is certainly true that unbelief is 100% a spiritual issue; no one becomes a Christian unless the Holy Spirit miraculously makes a dead heart alive. And yet, the Holy Spirit works through means. Look at the words that are used to describe the apostle Paul's evangelism in the book of Acts:

> Yet Saul grew more and more powerful and baffled the Jews living in Damascus by proving that Jesus is the Messiah. (9 v 22)

> Every Sabbath he reasoned in the synagogue, trying to persuade Jews and Greeks. (18 v 4)

> Paul entered the synagogue and spoke boldly there for three months, arguing persuasively about the kingdom of God. (19 v 8)

Paul fully relied on the person and work of the Holy Spirit, and yet still he reasoned, argued and proved.

Here's what that doesn't mean. Reasoning doesn't mean being "rationalistic": putting reason as our final judge or authority. God speaking through his word is our final authority. Arguing doesn't mean being "argumentative" like characters on a day-time television talk show.

But every Christian is called to "give a reason" for hope (1 Peter 3 v 15). This not merely an intellectual exercise, as if we are just brains on sticks. Nor is it a vague, airy-fairy "maybe" hope. It's a confident "living hope" (1 Peter 1 v 3). It's the kind of hope that engages all of who we are: our emotions, intellect, will, desire and imagination. We are whole people talking to other whole people and introducing them not to a philosophy or a worldview or even a message (although the gospel is all three) but a person. The old King James translation of Acts 8 v 35 gets this sense well:

> Then Philip opened his mouth, and began at the
> same scripture, and preached unto him Jesus.

But what's any of this got to do with engaging with culture?

The point is that sin and unbelief manifest themselves differently in different cultures and sub-cultures. Academics call this a "plausibility structure"— essentially, a worldview:

> A plausibility structure is a web of beliefs that are so
> embedded in the hearts and minds of the bulk of a
> society that people hold them either unconsciously
> or so firmly that they never think to ask if they are
> true ... One of the main functions of a plausibility

structure is to provide the background of beliefs that makes arguments easy or hard to accept.[5]

You don't need to be an academic to get this. We experience it every single day. The good news of Jesus Christ is deeply *implausible* in our culture at the moment. It's not that most people have spent endless hours studying Christianity and then decided that it's not for them. It's not that they've necessarily had a bad experience of Christians in the past which has turned them off (although some have). Rather, it's that the cultural air they've breathed in all their lives has shaped them to assume that Christianity is irrelevant, untrue and intolerant. And that's why we often hit a brick wall in our evangelistic efforts, and are left scratching our heads as to how we can ever get past first base with people. Our culture is such that Jesus is so far down people's agenda that he's not even an option to consider, much less one to accept.

This cultural change in air temperature affects the way we do evangelism. In 1989, with 29,000 others, I sat in the Crystal Palace football stadium, on the front row, to hear Billy Graham preach on the wealth of Solomon. Do I think I'll be engaged in this kind of evangelistic opportunity again in my lifetime? Sadly, the answer is no. At every West Ham home game, as thousands approach the London stadium, we pass a man standing on a box, shouting out Bible verses through a megaphone. Have I ever seen anyone engage with this man in any way? Sadly, the answer is no. Am I denying this man's faith or the power of the Spirit if I think there are more effective ways to proclaim the gospel?

To put it another way, and a little flippantly, we want to help people to meet the VIP Jesus Christ, but there are these big scary bouncers getting in the way, all bald heads and neck tattoos. Until we can get past them, introductions to Jesus can't be made. *And precisely what these "bouncers" are depends on a person's culture.*

I'll illustrate.

When I'm lecturing on this culture stuff, I sometimes pretend I'm the TV mind reader Derren Brown, because I can guess the objections that the audience's non-Christian friends have. But this isn't really mind reading: it's based on the principle that, roughly speaking, "I like people who are like me" (which means that most of my friends end up being like me). So in a room of mainly white, middle-class Christians, I know that their friends' objections will be things to do with science, miracles, evil, religious hypocrisy, sexuality and so on. I'm spookily accurate.

Here's the thing: I know that if I spoke to a group of Christians from a Muslim background, their friends would give a whole set of different objections. I've never heard a middle-class white British man say Christianity can't be true because of American foreign policy!

So to effectively engage our friends with the gospel— to give them a "reason" they'll find reasonable—we need to understand exactly what their unspoken assumptions are, and how we can get round them. And to identify their assumptions, we have to understand their worldview.

And how can we figure out what a person's worldview is? By looking at the cultural stories they consume and create.

As an example, it might be helpful to focus on what is probably the most pervasive worldview we encounter in the West today: secularism. The word "secular" is notoriously difficult to define, and academics (yes, them again!) spend a lot of time arguing over its meaning. However, the best analyses I've come across say that our secular age is not so much about declining church attendance, or even the question of whether religion should have a place in the public square and in politics. Our secular age is not about what people believe or don't believe, but more about what is *believable*. It's about believability. Christianity, and religion in general, is questioned and contested in a way that it just wasn't hundreds of years ago. It's now one option among many which are equally contested, and *that includes atheism*. Every option has its strengths and weaknesses, and we end up caught like a rabbit in the headlights.

As a result, one of the features of our secular culture is that people are disorientated and ill at ease. It's the spiritual equivalent of searching online for the best restaurant in our town and finding there are ten possibilities. Every single one has at least one one-star review. As a result, we become perpetually uncertain and increasingly anxious, or as one philosopher labels it, "fragilised".[6]

Part of this is all about trust. We know that life thrives on trust; we want to trust people and are nostalgic for days when parents could let kids play in the street. However, we are perpetually confronted with stories of adults and authorities abusing trust. We know we let ourselves down and so we ask whether we can trust anyone? As a result, we end up with guarded trust: we become obsessed with security and safety (when statistically we are safer than ever), always aware of abused trust and longing for true trust. This is not a comfortable place to be. Of course, there are those willing to cash in on this culture of distrust. Have you watched the advertisements between kids' shows on daytime television recently? For as many commercials as there are selling toys, there are loads selling insurance, or advertising lawyers asking whether you've been in an accident, with the promise of compensation (no win no fee, of course!).

It's important to note that this sense of disorientation isn't limited to those outside the church. Whether we like it or not, secularism is the framework for unbelief *and belief*: we all live in the secular age. *Even as Christians*, we inhale this worldview as we consume culture day by day. For example, how do we decide to trust (or not) the teaching of the pastor in a world of a million podcasts? We need to be honest and shift our thinking from seeing the "secular" as simply being "out there" to understanding it as the cultural context in which we follow Christ and tell others about him.

There is hope though. These bouncers I've been talking about are a bit like your average school bully. They talk a good game, but that's what they are: all talk. Prod them in the tummy and they'll double up. The reason? Generally speaking, many non-Christians have assumed their objections without ever questioning them in detail. A little poking and prodding will show this.

For every passionate atheist like Richard Dawkins or Stephen Fry, there are multitudes of those who might call themselves atheists or agnostics, but who can't quite fully accept that this "life under the sun" is all that there is: those who have no time for Christianity, but who still want to believe in significance, meaning, love, and even transcendence—a spiritual level beyond what we can see. Those who daily read their horoscopes or talk about what was or wasn't "meant to be". Those who might actually be called "religious" because they're certainly worshipping *something*.

It's summed up in the poignant opening of Julian Barnes' book *Nothing to Be Frightened Of*: "I don't believe in God but I miss him".

In a culture where we often think no one's interested in our message, we do in fact have an evangelistic way in. But we need to know where to look.

### 4. We care about Jesus!

Our last reason is perhaps the most important. Maybe it should have come first on the list. We engage with culture because we care about Jesus.

Who is Jesus Christ? He is the one to whom "all authority in heaven and on earth has been given" (Matthew 28 v 18). He is both *our* Lord and the Lord of the universe. The theologian and Dutch Prime Minister Abraham Kuyper was spot on when he said, "There is not a single inch in the whole domain of our human existence over which Christ, who is Sovereign over all, does not cry: 'Mine!'"[7] Jesus Christ has the right to be

Lord of all. His is "the name that is above every name" (Philippians 2 v 9). He does not accommodate or adapt himself to any culture; rather he reclaims it all because it's all legitimately his.

As for us, we are his ambassadors and vice-regents. Christians have a duty to challenge areas where Jesus' rule is not respected. Stories about anything in creation that do not relate that something to Christ are always incomplete and, to that extent, misleading. For that reason, "we demolish arguments and every pretension that sets itself up against the knowledge of God, and we take captive every thought to make it obedient to Christ" (2 Corinthians 10 v 5).

And that starts with working to make our own thoughts obedient to Christ for the sake of his glory. Not just the obviously "wrong" thoughts on lust and love but *all* of them. Our thoughts on money, family, government—all the assumptions our culture feeds us day by day that in reality are contrary to Christ, if only we could see it.

So we engage with culture because we're compelled to contend for Christ's honour—we want him to get the glory he deserves.

## BUT HOW?

Engaging with culture concerns our view of who we are as human beings, our Christian discipleship, our witness and evangelism. Most of all, it concerns the lordship of Jesus Christ. Nothing is more important than that.

Engaging with culture is essential—so how do we go about actually doing it?

Before we can take apart the counterfeit cultural stories that we consume every day, the first step is to have our hearts and imaginations captured by a truer and better story—the Bible's story. That's where we're heading next.

# 2. THE STORY OF CULTURE

One series that has been popular in the Strange household in the last few years has been the cooking competition *Masterchef Australia*. It's not to everyone's tastes, of course—and I mean that literally: some of us prefer eating braised pork belly to watching people cook braised pork belly. But the series is worth watching if only for what I call the Dessert-Dropping Moments. Audible gasps are heard from the sofas as, after hours and hours spent following a detailed recipe, a contestant's ridiculously complex and pretentious dessert is reduced to a sticky mess on the floor in a matter of moments.

In the last chapter we had a very quick introduction to what culture is and why we should care. Now we'll slow it down to look at the role of culture within the Bible's big storyline.

And there's an almighty Dessert-Dropping Moment coming.

## RULE: HUMAN BEINGS AS CULTURE-BUILDERS

Let's start by winding back to creation. In the first chapter of Genesis, we watch as out of nothing, God creates a vast array of good things. It's not as though God was lonely, twiddling his thumbs—he didn't need to create anything. And yet he did so with a remarkable creativity. The variety is amazing: light and dark, wet and dry, "great creatures" and "teeming" life forms. God speaks, and it all comes into existence. But he saves the best till last—the real highlight of his creation is you and me:

> Then God said, "Let us make mankind in our image,
> in our likeness, so that they may rule over the fish
> in the sea and the birds in the sky, over the livestock
> and all the wild animals, and over all the creatures
> that move along the ground."
>
> So God created mankind in his own image,
>   in the image of God he created them;
>   male and female he created them.
>
> (Genesis 1 v 26-27)

Very briefly, being made in God's image is about *revealing* who God is; *relating* to God, to each other and to the rest of creation; and *representing* God. So in these early chapters of Genesis, God reveals himself to be a speaker and maker, and as his image-bearers we too speak and make. That's the very first thing that Adam does:

> Now the LORD God had formed out of the ground
> all the wild animals and all the birds in the sky. He
> brought them to the man to see what he would

name them; and whatever the man called each living
creature, that was its name. So the man gave names
to all the livestock, the birds in the sky and all the
wild animals.                    (2 v 19-20)

It's like an early classificatory system. And a few verses
later, Adam composes the first ever poem upon seeing his
stunning new companion, Eve:

This is now bone of my bones
  and flesh of my flesh;
she shall be called "woman",
  for she was taken out of man.        (2 v 23)

So Adam is both the original science geek and arty-farty!

But in case we are in any doubt as to what being made
in the image of God might mean, in Genesis 1 v 28 and
2 v 15 God gives an explicit command to Adam and Eve.
Theologians call this the "cultural mandate":

Be fruitful and increase in number; fill the earth and
subdue it. Rule over the fish in the sea and the birds
in the sky and over every living creature that moves
on the ground.                    (1 v 28)

The LORD God took the man and put him in the
Garden of Eden to work it and take care of it.

(2 v 15)

Adam and Eve are to fill and subdue the earth, and to work
and keep the garden. At the heart of this is the notion of
"rule" or "dominion", an idea which is later picked up on
in Psalm 8:

> You have made them a little lower than the angels
> and crowned them with glory and honour.
> You made them rulers over the works of your hands;
> you put everything under their feet.   (Psalm 8 v 5-6)

God's images have the role of royal deputy. We image God's kingship in our kingship over creation. Yet what's really exciting is that this is not static—it involves development.

Imagine coming downstairs on one childhood Christmas morning and ripping the paper off an enormous, intricately designed model railway. It's all built and ready for you to play with. You get to press the "on" switch and adjust the speed, and watch the trains go round and round... and round... and round. This is fun for a while, but eventually it gets boring. Now imagine instead being given an amazing model railway to enjoy, *and* being given an infinite number of pieces of track and miniature scenery to keep expanding it. That's when model railways *really* become fun.

In the same way, Adam and Eve are charged with bringing out the potential of the creation (the "work" bit of 2 v 15), but they are to do so in a way that respects and nurtures God's original design (the "take care" bit).

Every human since is called to do the same thing: to rule over and develop creation by speaking and making, as we mirror our speaking and making God. And this, ultimately, is what we're doing when we create culture. Whether we're building skyscrapers or apps, writing a two-hour symphony or a two-sentence tweet, cooking food or watching a TV programme *about* cooking food—

big or small, from the sublime to the seemingly trivial, it is all speaking and making in the image of God.

Culture is a calling. It isn't something we do just to fill the time between clocking off from work and going to bed. It's something we do as part of being made in the image of God—and that's true of every human being, whether they realise it or not. And like everything else in creation, all of our culture-making has an ultimate purpose—to glorify God. We show off *his* greatness by pointing to *his* creativity. And living under God's norms and doing his work are the way we are glorified too. It's the way we flourish as human beings. It's how we find the sense of identity and significance we're all looking for.

## RUINED: HUMAN BEINGS AS CULTURE-DESTROYERS

And yet, most of us know that while everything God spoke and made in Genesis 1 was "good", there's plenty that humans speak and make that is not good. And I'm not just talking about the *Star Wars* prequels. I'm talking about the vicious comments of an internet troll, or the get-laid-quick philosophy behind Tinder, or the lies printed in a newspaper about a public figure, or the addiction that fuels our Netflix binges. Everyone senses that these things are "not good". In fact, almost all the culture we consume is tainted to one degree or another by the "not good". Why?

Well, we only have to flick forward a few pages in Genesis to find out. One of the ways to describe what happens in Genesis 3, in what Christians call the fall, is that creation is put into reverse. It's a tragic story—a real

"Dessert-Dropping Moment". Adam and Eve choose to disobey God and eat the fruit he commanded them not to. Instead of laying more track in God's cosmic model railway, they start snapping it in two and stamping on the figurines. Instead of reflecting God, they want to *be* God. As a consequence, the order and relationships between God, humans and the rest of creation that we see in the first two chapters of Genesis are undone.

### Two sides

What does this do to human culture-makers and their products? In Genesis 3 v 15, God tells the snake—Satan, who deceived Adam and Eve—what he is about to do:

And I will put enmity
between you and the woman,
and between your offspring and hers,
he will crush your head,
and you will strike his heel.          (Genesis 3 v 15)

Despite Eve's rebellion, there is hope that one of her offspring—Jesus Christ—will destroy the devil (Galatians 4 v 4). The stage is set for an all-out war. And like a war, this goes beyond a one-on-one combat. The consequences are far-reaching: this verse hints at two streams of humanity diametrically opposed to one another. And note that it is God himself who puts this hatred between the two! We see the fallout almost immediately in Genesis 4, as Adam and Eve's son Cain murders his own brother Abel. This stark this-or-that division continues all the way through the Bible; and as we read on in Scripture's storyline, we discover more of what it means. Satan's spiritual children are all those who live in rebellion against God. Eve's spiritual children are all those who live under God's rule, in the way humanity was meant to live from the start.

The New Testament records this difference in a whole host of vivid descriptions: every one of us is either in darkness or in light; a goat or a sheep; of the evil one or children of God. Ultimately, Genesis 3 v 15 points to the offspring of Eve who would crush Satan's head at the cross—Jesus Christ. You're either in Christ or you're not. There are no spiritual shades of grey; there is only black or white.

And what is it that distinguishes Satan's spiritual children from Eve's spiritual children? It's not a matter of what we do. It goes much deeper: right down to the human heart. In biblical terms, the heart is *the* core of the human person and the thing which determines our outward actions: "As water reflects the face, so one's life reflects the heart" (Proverbs 27 v 19). Jesus states that "where your treasure is, there your heart will be also" (Matthew 6 v 21). The problem is that ever since the fall, our hearts are on the wrong side. We're Satan's spiritual children—until, that is, God's gracious intervention enables us to change sides.

If being made in the image of God means we are built for worship, then there is a "heart's desire" intrinsic to being human which means we all worship—we were created to worship the living God, but we end up worshipping something else. It's worshipping this "something else" that the Bible calls idolatry. There are no alternatives to these two options: we worship God or we worship idols. Colossians 2 v 6-8 describes these two forms of existence in this way:

> So then, just as you received Christ Jesus as Lord, continue to live your lives in him, rooted and built up in him, strengthened in the faith as you were taught, and overflowing with thankfulness. See to it that no one takes you captive through hollow and deceptive philosophy, which depends on human tradition and the elemental spiritual forces of this world rather than on Christ.

There are those who are "rooted and built up *in [Christ]*," and those who are captive to "hollow and deceptive philosophy, which depends on human tradition and the elemental spiritual forces *rather than on Christ*". Two options: in Christ, or not in Christ.

So, we can say that culture is the dynamic way human beings shape the world around us as we make and speak in the image of God. But culture is also the "fruit" of our "root" heart relationship with God—and for most of humanity, that relationship is in a state of war. It's worth listening here to the American theologian John Frame, who gets this really well:

> Culture is what a society has made of God's creation, together with its ideals of what it ought to make. Or maybe we should put the ideal first. People make things, because they already have a plan in view, a purpose, a goal, an ideal. The ideal

comes first, then making things ... So now we can
see how culture is related to religion. When we
talk of values and ideals, we are talking religion.
In the broad sense a person's religion is what
grips his heart most strongly, what motivates
him most deeply ... It is interesting that the Latin
term "colere" ... also refers to religious service, and
comes into English as cult, cultic and so on. Culture
and cult go together. If a society worships idols,
false gods, that worship will govern the culture of
that society. If a society worships the true God,
that worship will deeply influence, even pervade its
culture. If like ours, a society is religiously divided,
then it will reveal a mixture of religious influences.[8]

Culture then is "religion externalised"—it's how we show
on the outside what we believe on the inside.[9] Culture is
how we worship—it's the way in which we show what is
really valuable to our hearts.

### We destroy culture

How then does our religious root affect our cultural fruit?
To understand this, it's first helpful to think of culture in
two ways.

First, culture is a description of what all human beings
do simply by being human. But second, "true", "real" and
"proper" culture is a prescription of what we should do
under God's original creation design and blueprint (even
though it will never be perfect this side of the new heaven
and new earth). The key is holding these two ideas in
tension. So let's unpack them.

The fact that we are deeply fallen and sinful human beings does not obliterate our image-of-God-ness. We can deny and vandalise God's image with our thoughts and actions, but ultimately, it's still this truth that makes human beings human beings. Moreover, God in his goodness often holds us back from ourselves so that we're not as bad as we could be. We call this God's common grace, and there are many blessings in it for which we are to be thankful. Therefore, however sinful we are, even after the fall, we are still human beings, and human beings produce "culture". God's creatures create from the creation around them. This is important because it means that however sinful or seemingly superficial a particular cultural form is, simply to dismiss or sneer at it without engaging with it in any way, shape or form, is implicitly to dismiss or sneer at one of God's broken image-bearers, who is worthy of dignity and respect. It's inhumane. Here's my theological hero Bavinck again:

> If only people could shed their self-awareness,
> their individuality, their sense of royalty; if only
> they could simply dissolve into the world around
> them like plants and animals do, without norms
> or morals! But they cannot. They are human. They
> exist with the indescribable greatness as well as the
> pathetic woefulness that that term covers. This is
> where God meets them.[10]

However, such fallen forms of culture can only be remnants or broken bits of "real culture", since they are products of broken images and sinful hearts. They are made in worship of an idol and not explicitly for God. Our culture-making after the fall cannot properly be called "real culture", because the values and purpose driving it are so radically different from those established in God's original good creation. Our sin has destroyed "real culture". All we're left with are the fragments.

## Culture destroys us

Yet at the same time, *we* are being destroyed by culture. Dominion over creation quickly becomes a horrible domination by the things we make. As we make and consume idolatrous culture, we breathe in a false story about who God is or isn't; who we are or aren't; what's gone wrong and how it can be put right. In our cultural creations, our false gods cunningly sell us "knocked off" false "gospel" stories, and we follow their scripts. Certainly, they look appealing, but they slowly kill us as we believe their lies and so lose our human identity. Worse, we become more and more distant from, and lose sight of, the God who created us for himself. It's a vicious cycle that spirals further and further from the truth.

So as we Christians look at the people around us, we can see that they both *make* culture and *are made* by it. Remember, culture is how our hearts worship idols. On the one hand, the Bible testifies in numerous places that idols are "made by human hands" (Psalm 135 v 15) and "nothing" (1 Corinthians 8 v 4) when compared to the living God. On the other hand though, they are "something"; they have the power to end up controlling the worshipper: "Those who make them will be like them, and so will all who trust in them" (Psalm 115 v 8). Greg Beale says that, throughout the Bible, "what people revere, they resemble, either for ruin or for restoration": we become what we worship.[11]

In Psalm 115, the idols "have mouths, but cannot speak, eyes, but cannot see" (v 5). Idol-worshippers become similarly blind and useless: "They know nothing, they understand nothing; their eyes are plastered over so that they cannot see, and their minds closed so that they cannot understand" (Isaiah 44 v 18).

And when do idol-worshippers look most like their lifeless objects of worship? When they're dead. Because that's where idol worship leads.

We see this two-way relationship on a bigger, society-wide level too. We are both influencers of culture and influenced by it. We sometimes get worried about relating our faith to stuff like politics and the public square, but "the public square is a battleground of the gods" and "people will always fight for their idols and gods, their objects of worship".[12] Laws can never save people, but they do shape people. Laws do affect those plausibility structures we thought about in the last chapter, if not for us, then for the next generation. It matters.

Remember: we become what we worship. For example, at the heart of the Islamic idea of God is the doctrine of *tawhid*—God is one, a monad, eternally alone (completely different from the unity of the Trinity in Christianity). Allah's transcendence, unknowability and power are stressed. Submission (which is what "Muslim" means) is key. If this is what Allah is believed to be like, then we shouldn't be surprised that for many Muslims, a vision of Islamic society will stress oneness over diversity, and submission over serving others. It's this principle that lies behind the Islamic concepts of *ummah* (the worldwide community of Muslims) and *dhimmitude* (the status of non-Muslims living in an Islamic country, who must pay extra taxes as a sign of submission).

So when it comes to culture, we must recognise the reality of the radical difference and cosmic conflict that rages between Satan's spiritual children and Eve's spiritual children. We really are in the middle of a culture war. This kind of language might sound too aggressive, pessimistic and defeatist to you. It's not very "nice". And yet it's language that the Bible uses so often. It accurately describes our spiritual situation. It's what we see before us when we put on the x-ray vision goggles of the Bible.

We need to be equipped to go into this cosmic culture clash—to make, shape and engage with culture for the sake of Christ. As we do so, we can know this: we're on the winning side—because the story doesn't end here.

## RESCUED, RESTORED AND RENEWED: JESUS CHRIST AS THE LORD OF CULTURE

One of my favourite Christmas carols that I love belting out is the G. F. Handel and Isaac Watts classic, "Joy to the World". However, my own joy is diminished when we often leave out the best verse!

No more let sin and sorrows grow,
Nor thorns infest the ground;

He comes to make his blessings flow
Far as the curse is found.

Jesus came to rescue us and the world from ruin. His redemptive work in the gospel isn't just about saving individual souls from hell—it is *cosmic* in scope. He's bringing about a new creation that is intimately related to the "in the beginning" creation: "Grace restores and perfects nature".[13]

When it comes to culture, Brian Mattson puts it nicely when he notes that the best stories have endings that resolve something that had potential from the beginning. In other words, if grace is our "happily ever after", it flows from nature's "Once upon a time":

> The perfection brought by Jesus Christ is a
> perfection God always intended for his creation.
> God's work of redemption after the fall was not a
> "Plan B". He did not change the plot or come up
> with something unrelated to his original purposes
> … The whole point of redemption is that God
> maintained his purposes for creation, so much—he
> so loved the world—that he was willing to die to
> make it happen.[14]

As we noted earlier, Adam woefully failed in his cultural task. Instead of caring for creation and extending the garden, his disobedience got him kicked out of the garden and brought God's curse upon the whole creation. But one of the titles and descriptions sometimes given to Jesus is the second or last Adam (e.g. 1 Corinthians 15 v 45). As the second Adam, Jesus succeeded in perfectly obeying his Father where the first man failed. Jesus Christ was the true image of God, without any cracks or stains of sin. He was the man of culture par excellence. He was anointed by the Spirit. He could still storms and raise the dead, demonstrating his perfect dominion over creation. And ultimately, Jesus' sacrificial death on the cross dealt with God's anger at our disobedience and reversed the curse. His resurrection was the firstfruits of the new creation—a taste of what is to come. His ascension into heaven means that today, he is our living and reigning Lord:

> The Son is the image of the invisible God, the firstborn over all creation. For in him all things were created: things in heaven and on earth, visible and invisible, whether thrones or powers or rulers or authorities; all things have been created through him and for him. He is before all things, and in him all things hold together. And he is the head of the body, the church; he is the beginning and the firstborn from among the dead, so that in everything he might have the supremacy. For God was pleased to have all his fullness dwell in him, and through him to reconcile to himself all things, whether things on earth or things in heaven, by making peace through his blood, shed on the cross.   (Colossians 1 v 15-20)

That, in a nutshell, is the gospel message. But what's that got to do with human culture and with us as Christians?

Here's the key idea: in the gospel, Christians are united to Jesus by faith, and we get our old job back. We are restored to our role as rulers over creation, because on our behalf, Jesus did what we couldn't, and now we are "in him".

In Christ, culture is our calling. Our new identity of being "in Christ" encompasses everything: "Whether you eat or drink or whatever you do, do it all for the glory of God" (1 Corinthians 10 v 31). The gospel of Jesus Christ confronts, reclaims and builds culture in a wonderful variety of ways, but which all conform to God's norms and for his glory.

As we are those who are united to Christ, his story of relating to culture becomes ours. It's a wonderful story, because ultimately it's about re-creation. It's about life and human flourishing and being part of a new world order, as Paul declares in 2 Corinthians 5 v 17: "Therefore, if anyone is in Christ, the new creation has come: the old has gone, the new is here!"

That re-creation starts with us, on a personal level. We are being remade and conformed to the image of Christ in our daily lives: "For those God foreknew he also predestined to be conformed to the image of his Son, that he might be the firstborn among many brothers and sisters" (Romans 8 v 29). And that's wonderful news, because to be conformed to Christ is to be made complete: "In Christ you have been brought to fullness" (Colossians 2 v 10). Everything is transformed and seen with new eyes. Our pain and suffering, while still real, sad, and often mysterious, is never pointless but serves the purpose of making us more like Christ (Hebrews 12 v 6). Even human death, that last enemy, becomes "ours"

(1 Corinthians 3 v 22). In the words of the Heidelberg Catechism, death "puts an end to our sinning and is our entrance into life."

But we're part of something bigger too. Christians are those who are filled by the Spirit of Christ and take up the cultural mandate originally given to Adam. We can play our part in the task he was given. But now the emphasis is different. Only Christ can redeem creation, but "in Christ" our good works become the means by which God extends his kingdom in the present. As faithful ambassadors of Christ, we actively proclaim his lordship, not by just looking back to the first creation but by looking forward to the new heaven and new earth, where this creation will be renewed and restored fully and for all eternity.

## KEEP IT REAL

When we know where we are placed in this big story, we can make sure we're "keeping it real" (yes, it is embarrassing when a middle-aged man says it!). The reality is that we are living after the resurrection but before Jesus returns. We're in the gap between the now (what Christ has already done) and the not-yet (what he will do one day).

We recognise that we live in a world groaning like a woman in labour (Romans 8 v 22). It's a world where we still suffer frustration, still toil: a world in which we still die. It's a "deny yourself, take up your cross and follow me" reality (Mark 8 v 34). It's a world where our cultural endeavours, even our greatest ones, are tainted with sin. This means a Christian cultural response should never be one that's "sugar-coated", "hunky-dory" or "pie in the sky". We must be careful we don't overdo the "now" and dial down the "not-yet".

Equally, we live in a reality of hope, joy and new life. We recognise that in the death and resurrection of Jesus, the world has been both turned around 180° and put the right way up. Jesus is Lord of the universe now. It's a "receiving a hundred times as much in this present age" reality (Mark 10 v 30). It's a world where individuals, families, communities and whole cultures can be transformed by the gospel. We must be careful that we don't overdo the "not yet" and dial down the "now".

We have been renewed, restored and retasked to take up the God-glorifying culture-building that we were created for. This is definitely not a distraction from evangelism. After all, how will other people be part of the new creation except by hearing the gospel message? Given the devastating effects of sin and the reality of hell, the call to repentance and faith in Christ remains at the centre of our mission, but in a way which is connected with our cultural calling. The way we "have dominion", "fill and subdue", and "tend and keep" in this new world order is for men, women and children to be converted. We are to go and make disciples of all nations.

The church also remains the bullseye of God's purposes, with its own distinctive role in cultural transformation. On behalf of the Lord Jesus Christ, Christians are engaged in a battle with the world. The gathered church is a heavenly army medical tent. Our church leaders are the field medics, strengthening us troops, treating our wounds after battle, feeding us with God's word and sending us back out into the world to take every thought captive for Christ.

Christians are engaged in a cosmic culture clash. But the key to winning in any combat is to know your opposition and to have a strategy to tackle it. That's what we're going to look at in the next two chapters.

# 3. CULTURE
# AS STORY

If you went onto the street and asked people what the answer is to the ultimate questions of life, the universe and everything—what do you think they'd say?

My guess is that you'd get lots of different answers (although sure, every smart alec who's actually got to the end of *The Hitchhiker's Guide to the Galaxy* would tell you it's 42).

Why are we here? What does it all mean? How can we be happy? What is right and wrong? What things in life are important? When it comes to answering these big, foundational questions, we all have a different idea— that's why culture, which expresses the answers, is so varied across different times and places. Remember our little definition of what culture ultimately is:

Culture is the stories we tell that express meaning about the world.

But here's the thing: the world around us already has a meaning. So what is it?

## GOD'S BIG REVEAL

As we've seen, being made in God's image means that because God is a speaker and a maker, so we too speak and make. Of course, depending on the status of our spiritual roots, our cultural fruit might be ripe or it might be rotten—but we all produce *something*. We can't do otherwise. It's what it means to be human. But it is *only* human.

What do I mean? Bluntly, our speaking and making can't be the same as God's speaking and making, because he is God and we are not! He is the Creator and we are mere creatures, part of the creation. This is an obvious but crucial distinction. God creates out of nothing. Before creation, there was only God: Father, Son and Holy Spirit. There was not even a speck of other stuff. But humans can't create out of nothing. At least, I know I can't.

So when we say that human beings "create" culture, we can only create out of existing materials. So in one sense, we don't really "create" anything. No, we are simply culture *builders*, building out of stuff that's already there. We might get to lay some track in God's awesome cosmic model railway, but we've got to be given the pieces first. In this sense, we can never make culture that is *truly* original, because only God can do that. Although human creativity can be totally mind-blowing, we are limited in our creativity because we are creatures and not the Creator.

Let's look a little more closely at the created materials with which we build culture—the stuff that inspires the stories we tell, the stuff out of which we make a home for ourselves in the world. Creation has God's fingerprints all over it. As with any great artist, you can tell it's his masterpiece just by looking at it. Creation means something even before we give it our own meaning. Creation tells us something about God and his identity. Creation is revelation, as David says in Psalm 19:

The heavens declare the glory of God;
    the skies proclaim the work of his hands.
Day after day they pour forth speech;
    night after night they reveal knowledge.

(Psalm 19 v 1-2)

So what exactly is the "knowledge" that the world around us reveals? It's helpful to think about what God reveals about himself in terms of shadows and sunbeams. Once we're clear on God's *true meaning* behind the world, that will help us make sense of the alternative "meanings" that human beings express through culture (we'll get to this second part a bit later).

### SHADOWS

Christians believe that history is heading somewhere. We believe in endings, in reckonings, in final justice. The Bible describes a Judgment Day when all of humanity will have to stand before God and give an account. Scripture's shorthand for this is the "day of God's wrath" (for example, in Zephaniah 1 v 15; Revelation 6 v 17).

The word "wrath" conjures up all kinds of images that have nothing to do with the Bible's definition. When the Bible talks about God's wrath, it doesn't mean an all-too-human, arbitrary, fly-off-the-handle rage. Rather, God's wrath is his divine, personal, settled, righteous anger. It's our holy God's revulsion and opposition to all evil. And note that it's Jesus Christ, the Lamb of God, who will be at the centre of proceedings on Judgment Day:

> Then the kings of the earth, the princes, the generals, the rich, the mighty, and everyone else, both slave and free, hid in caves and among the rocks of the mountains. They called to the mountains and the rocks, "Fall on us and hide us from the face of him who sits on the throne and from the wrath of the Lamb! For the great day of their wrath has come, and who can withstand it?"     (Revelation 6 v 15-17)

Those not in the "Lamb's book of life" (Revelation 13 v 8) will face the "wrath of the Lamb". This frightening picture is intended to be a wake-up call to us all. However, what's even more frightening is that there are so many people sleeping through this alarm. Paul warns both Jews and non-Jews in his letter to the Romans:

> But because of your stubbornness and your unrepentant heart, you are storing up wrath against yourself for the day of God's wrath, when his righteous judgment will be revealed.   (Romans 2 v 5)

Imagine a big canvas, stretched out to give shelter to those underneath. Over time gallons and gallons of water are poured onto this sheet and it starts to collect. It gets heavier and heavier, and the sheet slowly starts to sag under the weight of all that water. Those underneath think everything is OK; there's no problem—they just roll over and go back to sleep. But in reality there's a *huge problem*, as that sheet gets heavier and heavier, and the water keeps on collecting. And then comes that awful moment when the whole thing comes crashing in. The day of God's wrath will be that cosmic crashing in.

But this isn't all there is to say about God's wrath. Earlier in Romans, we read that "the wrath of God is being revealed from heaven against all the godlessness and wickedness of people, who suppress the truth by their wickedness" (Romans 1 v 18). Yes, there is a final day of wrath, but all humanity experiences God's wrath *now* too. It's as if God has taken out a penknife and has cut a little slit in the canvas, and "drops of wrath" are falling down below.

Why would God make these cuts? It sounds bleak, but it's actually a gracious warning sign. These "drops of wrath" are God telling us that something has gone terribly wrong, and we need to do something about it. We need to listen up and turn around before it's too late. The day of his wrath is a clear and present danger—the "threat level" is critical. And God tells us about it in lots of ways. It's in the little things—the stubbed toe and the broken phone. Or in the reality that your living room gets messy, but it never "gets tidy" without your intervention.

It's in the big things too. He tells us about it in all the frustration and brokenness and dysfunction we see in the world, in all the ways we go against God's design for humanity. We see it in disaster and disease and dishonesty. Supremely, we see it in human death. Consider these words from Psalm 90:

All our days pass away under your wrath;
  we finish our years with a moan.
Our days may come to seventy years,
  or eighty, if our strength endures;
yet the best of them are but trouble and sorrow,
  for they quickly pass, and we fly away.
If only we knew the power of your anger!
  Your wrath is as great as the fear that is your due.

(Psalm 90 v 9-11)

The simple fact that we all die is a warning sign of God's wrath. Like Adam and Eve, we want to be "like God", but we quickly find out that our days are numbered.

I may be unusual, but I've never had a non-Christian friend rush up to me and say that they woke up that morning feeling heavy under the wrath of God. But the Bible tells me that they experience God's wrath every day, even though they may not realise it. And it's this "felt wrath" that they tell me about. It's all the frustration and futility that they think life or fate has thrown at them: the terrible traffic, the school bullies, the bad back, the failed business, the cancer diagnosis. It's a huge shadow cast back from the end of the world. *It's a taste of hell on earth*. It's all meaningful because it's God's message to us. And it demands a response. This is what Jesus is getting at in Luke 13 v 1-5:

Now there were some present at that time who told Jesus about the Galileans whose blood Pilate had mixed with their sacrifices. Jesus answered, "Do you think that these Galileans were worse sinners than all the other Galileans because they suffered this way? I tell you, no! But unless you repent, you too will all perish. Or those eighteen who died when the tower in Siloam fell on them—do you think they were more guilty than all the others living in Jerusalem? I tell you, no! But unless you repent, you too will all perish."

The shadows we experience in this life warn us of God's wrath, and tell us to repent before it's too late.

## SUNBEAMS

It's not only shadows though—there are sunbeams too. Yes, Christians believe in the day of wrath and the reality of hell, but we also believe in an amazing new heaven and new earth—a place where there will be only blessing and joy. There will be a total absence of evil, pain and mourning. It's described in Revelation like this:

I heard a loud voice from the throne saying, "Look! God's dwelling-place is now among the people, and he will dwell with them. They will be his people, and God himself will be with them and be their God. 'He will wipe every tear from their eyes. There will be no more death' or mourning or crying or pain, for the old order of things has passed away."

He who was seated on the throne said, "I am making everything new!"                (Revelation 21 v 3-5)

And these blessings and joys are not only a future experience. In his "common grace", we see God's lavish goodness shown to all creation now: "He causes his sun to rise on the evil and the good, and sends rain on the righteous and the unrighteous" (Matthew 5 v 45). This common grace is all the wonderful things in creation, including the wonderful things human beings are capable of, that we experience now. It's everything that speaks of order, love, desire, beauty, wisdom and "rightness". These are sunbeams—dancing rays of light pointing upwards to the source of all goodness: God himself. These gifts of grace are to be interpreted as such. They are to be received with thanksgiving. And so like the shadows, the sunbeams are God telling us something.

Again, I may be unusual, but I've never had a non-Christian friend rush up to me and say that they woke up that morning feeling the joy of being alive and wanting to thank God for their life and breath and everything. But the Bible tells me that they experience God's blessing every day, even though they may not realise it. And it's this "felt blessing" that they tell me about in all their excitement about the new relationship, the big promotion or the amazing holiday. It's a sunbeam flaring out from the sun. *It's a taste of heaven on earth.* It's all meaningful because it's God's message to us.

And like most important messages, it demands a reply. So how do we respond?

## RESPONSE #1: SUPPRESSION

So God speaks to us in his creation (and he speaks *through* us, as we ourselves are part of this creation). In shadows, God tells us that something is not right and we need to turn around. In sunbeams, God calls us to respond to him in thankfulness and praise.

Job done? Sadly not. How do we respond to God's megaphone? In an understatement, not well.

The wrath of God is being revealed from heaven
against all the godlessness and wickedness of people,
who suppress the truth by their wickedness.

(Romans 1 v 18)

Like someone violently holding a person's head under the water in order to drown them, we suppress the truth. In our rebellion against God, we try and squash it, squish it, stamp on it. We get a big fat marker pen and graffiti all over it.

How though? The God-given meanings built into creation are given new meanings in the culture we build. So the pain, terror and unnaturalness of the shadow of death, which is God telling us that something is wrong, is now reinterpreted as the smooth process of "crossing over" from one realm to another. Don't be afraid: death is perfectly natural, it's to be embraced. It's nothing to be scared of. We see this portrayal of death in a lot of popular culture. One of 2015's biggest singles—"See you again" by Wiz Khalifa and Charlie Puth—made death sound almost serene, as you follow a light and hold on to your memories.

The other way we suppress the truth about death is to simply ignore the topic completely and not mention it in polite company. What's especially tragic is that people often decide to interpret human suffering as evidence that God either doesn't care or doesn't exist—the very opposite of God's real meaning. The presence of suffering in our world is a painful but ultimately loving warning that is intended to lead us to repentance, and save us from far greater suffering beyond death.

In the same way, those beautiful sunbeams which are meant to issue in thanks and praise are completely turned on their heads. I remember once speaking at a weekend away for Christians at a prestigious music college. The issue that these Christians struggled with most was the culture of competition, which was all around them and which they found hard to resist. The students in that college had been given the most amazing musical gifts. The result of receiving these gifts should have been thanksgiving—pointing to God, the giver of all good gifts. The purpose of these gifts should have been to bring pleasure to others. However, the students ended up using their gifts to only point inwards and foster a selfish pride and ambition which would stop at nothing to get ahead of fellow students. They had turned the sunbeams into shadows.

The problem is not that God's communication is ineffective; it's that human beings are so rebelliously sinful that we are determined not to listen to it. God speaks to us, but we end up speaking over God. And this isn't a one-off. It's not a static thing. This relationship is very dynamic. Have you ever played the game at the beach when you try to sit on a beachball in the sea? You try really hard to get that ball under the water and you nearly succeed, but then at the last second it pops up again two feet away, and you have to start again. So it is with God's revelation and our response. We suppress the truth, but we can never totally suppress the truth. Reality keeps getting in the way. The real world doesn't quite seem to be the right shape to fit our hole, and so there's a horrible grating sound as we apply force to push it through.

Another reason that the truth keeps bursting through is that we are made in God's image, and so we speak and make only as creatures. We can't even make stories out of nothing! That's why throughout history there seem to be perennial questions, themes and plots that storytellers are attracted to time and time again—the search for love, riches to rags and rags to riches, heroic self-sacrifice, the quest for home. One theologian calls them "magnetic points"—primal questions to which we are irresistibly attracted.[15] All these stories are mere echoes of the gospel story.

The image of God is like one of those inextinguishable birthday candles you get from a joke shop. We can try and blow it out. We can lick our fingers to snuff it out. We can get a jug of water to throw on it. We can strap dynamite to it and try to blow it up—but it will not die. It keeps flickering back into flame. And so there are times, however fleeting, when we see in culture the message of shadows and sunbeams getting through: when God's voice is heard over our shouting.

God keeps on revealing himself, and we keep on suppressing the message. And so we are "without excuse" (Romans 1 v 20)—we know the truth; we just don't want to hear it.

## RESPONSE #2: SUBSTITUTION

Not only do we suppress the truth, but we substitute other things for the truth, as Paul goes on to write:

> For although they knew God, they neither glorified him as God nor gave thanks to him, but their thinking became futile and their foolish hearts were darkened. Although they claimed to be wise, they became fools and exchanged the glory of the immortal God for images made to look like a mortal human being and birds and animals and reptiles.
>
> (Romans 1 v 21-23)

When we push truth down, we fill the gap with god-substitutes. This is what the Bible calls idolatry. Idolatry turns "good things" into "god-things". Being made in God's image means we are instinctive worshippers. So when we try to smother reality, we end up making new twisted realities which we are devoted to instead.

Think about having a nightmare. Often our nightmares are made up of ordinary things we've encountered during the day, which take on an extraordinary life of their own as we sleep. They are bent out of all proportion and become monstrous and grotesque, like an image in a fairground hall of mirrors.

This is precisely what idolatry is. The idolatry complex takes a good thing in creation and inflates and distorts it to be a functional god. Culture is what we make when lots of us are having the same twisted fantasy. Idols spin and conjure a false gospel story and promise the world but ultimately only deliver disillusionment, despair and destruction. Most importantly, idolatry is always ultimately against God and against the way he has chosen to reveal himself to us.

God's shadows and sunbeams are meant to be signs and pointers to eternal realities. That cold drip, drip, drip on our face is meant to warn us. That warm sunbeam on our face is meant to bring our thanks. However, when in our nightmares these signs are disconnected from what they signify, then they end up pointing to themselves. They take the place of God. It's the equivalent of thinking that the appetiser is actually the main course. When all our culture's hopes, fears, desires, longings and identities only point to the *now* of the immediate reality before our eyes, without any sense of a not-yet, then something has gone badly wrong.

God's shadows tells us there is something wrong in the world and wrong with humanity, and deep, deep down we know this, but the stories and scripts our culture weaves in books, TV, films and social media are delusional fantasies. Author Grant Horner puts it nicely:

We cling to utterly unrealistic views about human nature, and we struggle with a recognition that "something is not right" with the world. From this most people tend to go in either of two directions: they become idealists detached from reality or they become cynics detached from humanity. Hence the two great classical genres of Comedy and Tragedy. Everything will work out in the former; everyone will die miserably in the latter. What will it be? "The Sound of Music" (1965) or

"Unforgiven"? Do we escape the Swiss Alps singing "Edelweiss", or do we die on the ballroom floor, rolling in blood and broken glass, dreaming of a house we'll never live in?[16]

And so in response to God's messages, our idolatrous suppression and substitution result in cultures of broken, fragmented stories. They create what appear to be highly plausible and ingenious imaginary worlds. But here's what is important to remember: idols are parasitic on the truth. They're like a counterfeit designer handbag—it *looks like* Gucci, but it's definitely *not* Gucci. Because these idolatrous stories are *counterfeit* stories, they hint at and glimmer with the truth and reality of God's revelation. However, ultimately these are fantastical nightmares, stories twisted horribly out of shape. Inhabiting them and following the script they give us takes us further away from reality, from ourselves and from our Creator. We need a wake-up call. We need a better story.

## WAKE UP!

There's probably contrary medical advice out there, but I'm always glad when my wife, Elly, has woken me up from a nightmare. It's a feeling of sheer relief when I hear the words, "Love, don't worry. It's only a nightmare. It's not real".

As Christians, we believe it's only the power of the gospel of Jesus Christ revealed in the Bible that can wake us up from our living nightmares and bring us back to reality. It's only the gospel that can bring sanity and turn the world the right way up. It gives us a whole new way of seeing and interpreting the world *as God himself sees it*, founded on the new life that Jesus brings in his life, death and resurrection. Remember, when we become Christians and are indwelled by the Spirit, the new creation has already begun in us. Now you and I have a role in amplifying God's message to the world around us.

The Bible does biting satire even better than *The Onion*. In Isaiah 40 – 55, the prophet gives a masterclass in comparing God, the Holy One of Israel, with the worthless idols built and worshipped by the surrounding nations. The big point is that there is no comparison. How could Israel ever be tempted to follow any other Lord when there is no other? Then in chapter 44 Isaiah ridicules the idolater who, out of one block of wood, makes both his god and the fire for his evening meal:

> They know nothing, they understand nothing;
>   their eyes are plastered over so that they cannot see,
>   and their minds closed so that they cannot
>   understand.
> No one stops to think,
>   no one has the knowledge or understanding to say,
>   "Half of it I used for fuel;
>   I even baked bread over its coals,
>   I roasted meat and I ate.          (Isaiah 44 v 18-19)

"No one stops to think." Most people I know don't think about culture, or worship, or ways of viewing the world, or idolatry, or felt wrath and felt grace. They are just living their lives. They're just scrolling through

Facebook. They're just watching TV. They don't stop to think. And it's part of our mission to get them to stop and think—to try and rouse them from their nightmare and bring them back to reality, back to their senses. The idols we worship can't and don't deliver what they promise on any level, whether intellectually, emotionally or imaginatively. They can't give satisfying ultimate explanations of the world.

Our task is to make people "stop and think" about their self-deception. To make them "stop and think" about the commitments they make, the authorities they listen to, the stories and scripts they follow. And from here it's only a short step to get to Jesus.

"No one stops to think." What about you? When did you last stop to think? About the film everyone's raving about, or the news article you just read, or the song you've got stuck in your head. Christians are not immune to the lure of these idolatrous stories. Remember the parting words of the apostle John to Christians in his first letter? "Dear children, keep yourselves from idols" (1 John 5 v 21). We spend our days submerged in these cultural stories—so we need to learn how to consume them intelligently. We need to learn to identify where they are suppressing the truth, and to spot where that truth keeps "popping up" like a beach ball. This is what it means to "engage with culture"—not to swallow its stories hook, line and sinker, but to let it point our own eyes over and over again to the gospel story.

We can both confront and connect the gospel to any and every broken story in our culture and every culture.

But how, exactly? That's what we'll be moving on to shortly. Before that though, we need to pause and tackle something that's always a little tricky.

# 4. "CAN I WATCH...?"

In a book on cultural engagement, with a chapter title like that, you may have already guessed the question...

As a Christian, is it OK for me to watch [insert generic TV show with sex and/or violence]?

You've probably been waiting for this chapter. Indeed, this might be the first one you've flicked through to read (I probably would have done the same myself!). I know that I've been putting off writing it. Because the short answer is, "It depends..." That might disappoint you: "Oh, thanks for nothing, Dan. You've fudged it." Well, just hear me out.

For a long time questions like "Can I watch...?" "Should I watch...?" and "How far is too far?" have created a lot of heat (and a lot of blog posts) in our Christian subculture. More recently much of it has revolved around shows like *Mad Men* and *Game of Thrones*. The various arguments have been rehearsed, responded to, re-rehearsed and re-responded to. I'm exhausted just following the conversation. If I read all the debate, I wouldn't have time to watch these shows, even if I wanted to!

The theological issues raised in this discussion are as old as the hills. It's the latest variation on the tension of being "in the world but not of the world". It's that delicate balance that ensures our Christian *liberty* doesn't become or sound like *licence*—permission to sin—or *legalism*—a focus on rule-keeping. Arguably it could be seen as a sign of health that we are having these discussions. I think they call it a "creative tension". What it does show is that a couple of proof texts, a blog post and some off-hand remarks are never going to settle such issues once and for all—every generation will articulate this struggle in their own way.

## WALKING THE TIGHTROPE

So why does it matter what we watch anyway? In chapter 2 we gave four reasons why we engage with culture. These are the reasons why we need to be thoughtful about what we watch (and read, play, buy, listen to and scroll through):

- As cultural consumers and creators, we've got no choice—we're surrounded by this stuff. We're always going to watch something.

- We care about our own discipleship and the discipleship of others—we want to honour Christ in how we live, and help others to do likewise.

- We care about telling others about Jesus so they become disciples—our cultural assumptions shape how we do this, and our cultural choices can be a helpful tool.

- As his ambassadors and vice-regents, we care about Jesus' Lordship over everything—he deserves to be glorified in every TV show, radio podcast and Instagram story.

When considered rightly, these four reasons can hold hands, play nicely and get along with each other very well. But they can also easily become detached from each other, so that we start focusing on one at the expense of the others. The key to wisely answering the "Can I watch?" question is to hold all four in tension.

Holding truths in tension is something we encounter again and again in Scripture. The apostle John, who says "Dear children, keep yourselves from idols" (1 John 5 v 21), and "Do not love the world or anything in the world" (2 v 15) is the same John who writes about Jesus engaging the Samaritan women right where she is (John 4), and who then later records Jesus praying about his disciples being sent *into* the world (17 v 18).

The apostle Paul writes about becoming "all things to all people so that by all possible means I might save some" (1 Corinthians 9 v 19-23). And yet he's the same apostle who time after time after time calls disciples to be wise in how they walk (Ephesians 5 v 15), to flee from sexual immorality (1 Corinthians 6 v 18), to keep God's commandments and the "law of Christ" (1 Corinthians 7 v 19; Galatians 6 v 2), and to "have nothing to do with the fruitless deeds of darkness, but rather expose them.

It is shameful even to mention what the disobedient do in secret" (Ephesians 5 v 11-12).

Jesus Christ, the Lord of all creation and Creator of every good gift—who was criticised for befriending tax collectors, prostitutes and foreigners, and who commands us to likewise make disciples of all nations—is the same Lord who warns that "anyone who looks at a woman lustfully has already committed adultery with her in his heart. If your right eye causes you to stumble, gouge it out and throw it away" (Matthew 5 v 28-29).

## WHAT "IT DEPENDS" DEPENDS ON

So, tension is normal. That means that knowing when legitimate cultural engagement and enjoyment is actually illegitimate cultural indulgence and idolatry is a matter of wisdom and discernment. How do you know what is OK to watch and what is not OK?

Well... it depends. There is no "one-size-fits-all" answer that means I can give you a hard and fast rule for every show or situation. Consider some of the things that "it depends" depends on.

First, everyone's *character* is different—we all have our own individual wiring. Whether we are female or male does have a bearing on this, although that isn't the whole of the matter. More precisely, we all have what Richard Lovelace calls our "characteristic flesh"—the particular ways in which we are prone to wander and deceive ourselves. And yes, we can be very adept in self-deception.

Second, everyone's *conscience* is calibrated differently with varying levels of sensitivity (more on this later).

Third, our *contexts* make a difference—both the wider culture we belong to and the unique web of relationships that make up our lives. For some of us it's harder than for others to avoid the muddy puddles, especially when those we love are up to their necks in it, wallowing around quite happily but slowly sinking deeper and deeper. Holding out a hand to pull them to safety always runs the risk of us getting our clothes spattered.

Finally, a healthy dose of sanctified *common sense* means that some judgment calls are easier than others. Money, sex and power are common areas we need to be careful in; we need to be vigilant in guarding our hearts to ensure we don't get sucked into the world's way of thinking in these areas. Actually, though, these are relatively obvious dangers. We also need to beware other areas that are more subtle but also harmful.

For example, most Christians are rightly concerned about the increasing sexualisation of our culture, but what about the *sentimentalisation* of our culture? Sentimentality is emotional self-indulgence, so that what you feel becomes most important. We often see it in the public reaction to the death of a celebrity. While apparently well-meaning, sentimentality is actually selfish. It directs our emotions to our own emotions, so we are always the main character of our story. Although it pretends to care for the "other", it really only cares for the self—the "other" merely becomes a means to an end (feeling something). Sentimentality allows us to experience shared public emotional expression, without the commitment of real-life relationships. As such, sentimentality is simplistic. It leaves little room for nuance, complexity and fortitude. The sentimental world consists of clear-cuts: of goodies and baddies, victims and perpetrators. Every situation demands an immediate answer.

Now doesn't this describe a myriad of reality TV shows and kids' "comedies" on the Disney Channel and Nickelodeon? We might think these types of shows are pretty innocent for us and our kids because they aren't full of sex, swearing and violence. But they are sickly sentimental and have a rotting effect, because they present a fantastical fake world which encourages us to feel in clichés. Or consider *The Greatest Showman*. At one level it is a family film with a feel-good message and catchy soundtrack. But its "feel-goodness" is part of the problem: it's all too easy. Things get patched up far too quickly with an emotional song, as the characters go back to dancing with CGI tigers at the end. Real life is messier.

This doesn't mean we should never watch these things or let our kids watch them, but we sometimes need to call them out. When these shows are on in our house, I shout out the word "bilge" at the offending moments.

There is a public and political side to all of this too. Sentimentality's pressure for simplicity and quick responses means that authorities can be bullied into quick fixes, and not the hard grind of reflecting on long-term solutions which would be genuinely caring. For all Ariana Grande's stadium rendition of "Somewhere over the rainbow" in the wake of 2017's Manchester Arena bombing says about solidarity and the importance of communal expressions of grief, it is not going to defeat Isis.

Am I being too cynical? Maybe. But the point is this: as we consume culture, sex is not the only danger we need to be aware of.

## FIVE THEOLOGICAL FOOTBALL CHANTS

If those are all the things that "it depends" depends on, how can we possibly come up with an actual answer for this or that artist or novel or TV show? Sometimes in thinking about this stuff, I feel I'm so far down the rabbit-hole that I'm totally disorientated. But there is a way to be pulled back out, to gain some perspective and see the wood, not just the trees: to be reset and reorientated. And it comes from an unlikely source.

You might remember that 2017 saw the 500th anniversary celebrations of the Reformation—a period of history when people all over Europe rediscovered the truths at the heart of the Bible. During that summer of 2017, I was asked to give a series of conference talks on the five Solas of the Reformation—five slogans featuring the word *sola* (Latin for "alone") which became a rallying cry for what it meant to be Protestant. Let's call them theological football chants: *Scripture alone, grace alone, faith alone, Christ alone, God's glory alone.*

At the time, I thought preparing this material would be a welcome 16th-century break from all this 21st-century "culture stuff" that I'm normally thinking about. To my surprise, as I prepped, I was struck by the relevance of these slogans to the whole cultural engagement topic. These precious truths, which are the heartbeat of our faith, can act as foundations, fences and flags for us. They are a useful test or filter through which to measure our cultural consumption and creation. I call these "Solas" our "only" option. Let's take them in turn.

## SCRIPTURE ALONE

"Scripture alone" declares that the Bible is our ultimate authority and that we must interpret the world through the word. This involves not just thinking *about* the Bible (although, of course, we must do that); it involves thinking *through* the Bible—thinking *biblically* about everything else. So it's not about cherry-picking verses, stories and isolated truths, but going deep—going "meta". The Bible has repeated structures and patterns which act like a pair of x-ray goggles that we put on to see *all* the world *all* the time as it *really* is. We've already been talking about some of those patterns in this book, but there are many others, lots of which are laid down at the beginning in Genesis.[17]

Unlike my daughter, who only wears her glasses for watching TV, we need to wear our x-ray goggles all the time, using them to look at and assess everything that human beings do. The author C.S. Lewis said, "I believe in Christianity as I believe that the sun has risen, not only because I see it, but because by it I see everything else".[18] Lewis was merely echoing the psalmist: "In your light we see light" (Psalm 36 v 9).

As we've already seen, if we're not looking at the world through the Bible's story, there are plenty of other "big stories" ready to hoodwink us. They're prowling around our society, looking to be master interpreters of the universe. More accurately, they are prowling "beneath" our society. To paraphrase a hit of recent years, it's *all about that bass*. These stories are drumming away under the surface; but we often miss them if we only stay above ground and listen to what just seems like a confused and random mess pouring out of our TV screens. These other "big stories" are influencing us to know what is important and why, to know and feel what is praiseworthy and blameworthy, and what sort of action is appropriate to promote the former and resist the latter. Again, we don't often think *about* these other stories because our culture thinks with them.

Sometimes, though, we get a peek of what's going on. I remember with some concern walking into my son's room after his first term of studying geography at university and seeing the books on his floor taken from the reading list he'd been given. Most of them were by the atheist Michel Foucault, whose big-theories on knowledge, power and sexuality have been hugely influential in our society, including in the study of geography. Certainly these same theories have influenced those in television, and other media and arts.

If we don't discern, articulate and persuade others with the Bible's blueprint for the flourishing of human life and culture, then others will... and are. And ultimately these alternative stories are all hope-less.

So when you're watching something, or wondering whether to watch it, ask yourself this:

- Why does everyone else seem to think this is good or important? What does that reveal about what they think is important or praiseworthy?

- Why do I enjoy this, or think I would enjoy it? What does that reveal about what I think is important or praiseworthy?

- How does this compare to the Bible's pattern? Does Scripture agree that these things are important or praiseworthy? Or are these messages coming from an alternative "big story"?

## GRACE ALONE

Grace alone reminds us that our acceptance before God is not based on anything we "do" but what God has "done" in Christ. We contribute nothing. We can't earn our salvation—it's a free gift.

What's the cultural relevance of this? It means that our reason for watching or not watching something needs to be grace focused. We should be wary about any rationale for "No" that puts imperatives (e.g. be holy) *before* indicatives (e.g. you *are* holy *in Christ*). This order matters. If I'm saved by grace alone, then the motive behind my cultural choices is not to keep rules to somehow impress God or prove myself worthy but to love and honour God because of what he's already done for me.

Second, something doesn't quite sit right when, in the tone of this culture debate, there's an angst about the survival of the church, or the risk of losing one's personal faith. It's almost as if we believe we need to take control of the wheel and do something urgently, because God has somehow drifted off. But if we're saved by grace, then it's *all* of God. He is sovereign, and he's got control of the ship; no TV show can steer us into an iceberg when our Father's at the helm. That's not to say that the New Testament doesn't warn us to be on our guard against sin—it does (for example, in Ephesians 5 v 3-6). We'll come to that later. But there is an opposite danger too. Mike Cosper gets it right when he says:

Grace shapes our encounters with the world by first promising that nothing will ever harm us eternally and second, by motivating us to better things, better standards, better ways of thinking about the things we encounter. Where the law motivates with the threat of punishment, grace motivates with the promise of joy. We can step into the world with a sense of invitation. This is our Father's world. What do we want to explore today?[19]

This means we can ask the questions:

- If, when considering this culture choice, my gut instinct is "no"—why is that? Is that rooted in an imperative or an indicative?

- Is it possible that I am being wrongly fearful, or am I seeking to enjoy living as my Father's child?

## FAITH ALONE

"Faith alone" reminds me of the means through which I am united to Christ and receive all his benefits—it is through faith alone.

These benefits include what John Calvin calls "double grace". First, through our initial faith we are reconciled to God—Christ's blameless record becomes our blameless record. Second, through our ongoing faith we are "sanctified by Christ's spirit [so that] we may cultivate blamelessness and purity of life".[20] Far from tiptoeing around simply trying to avoid evil, our living faith spurs us to pursue good works that spill out into our churches and communities, bringing blessings to individuals, families and society at large: "You, my brothers and sisters, were called to be free. But do not use your freedom to indulge the flesh; rather, serve one another humbly in love" (Galatians 5 v 13). Our good works include our cultural endeavours, which are part of the way we have dominion and fill and subdue the earth. Remember, we are not simply consumers but creators.

Consider this. In the "Can I watch?" debate, one of the reasons we might be willing to put up with unhelpful aspects of a particular TV show or film is the pay-off of what's good about it: the amazing skill in complex and subtle storytelling and screenplays, or incredible artistic world-building which makes us gasp. I'd like to ask some hard questions here: Could it be that because our own cultural cupboards are bare, our starving imaginations are forced to live off the world's scraps? Are we always consuming culture and never creating it? Why aren't *we* telling better stories with all the same realism, imagination, subtlety, complexity and beauty, but without those aspects which make it difficult and unhelpful for us? Why aren't we strategically locating, discipling, resourcing and sending out Christians gifted in the arts and the media? [21]

It can start with you. Write a poem, hum a tune, doodle a picture, imagine a plotline, draft a screenplay. To create rather than just consume will mean making conscious choices. There are only twenty-four hours in a day. We will need to prioritise. Our social-media habits will need to be carefully examined so we are less distracted and more disciplined in exercising our minds.[22] But our hungry imaginations will thank us for the feast.

So as you consider a particular cultural choice ("Can I watch [insert title here]?"), ask yourself:

- What is the "pay-off" that you want to enjoy about this thing? Is there a way you could create culture which celebrates that good thing, without the need to compromise?

- How could you carve out time to do more cultural creation? How might you encourage your brothers and sisters to do the same?

## CHRIST ALONE

Christ alone declares that salvation is achieved only by Christ's death and resurrection—he's the mediator we need between ourselves and God.

As we've said in previous chapters, we are creatures made in God's image, designed for an eternal relationship with him, and built for transcendence. Although the world around us suppresses this truth by arguing that life "under the sun" is all that there is, we can never eradicate our sense of the divine. It will pop up in everything that humans make. We see this all over the place when we look hard enough. The secular is indeed haunted by this longing for a deeper meaning. Despite the rhetoric, it's never easy to consistently speak and act as if this material world is all that there is.

However, "Christ alone" means we mustn't get carried away with this insight. Yes, our culture will always be looking for something else. But unless the search finds its fulfilment in the Jesus Christ of the Scriptures, then it remains stuck in a world of idolatry. A vague sense of "transcendence", "faith", "spirituality" and even "theism" isn't enough, because salvation comes through faith in Christ alone. People might be "seeking" God (Acts 17 v 27), but their seeking is like the blinded cyclops who groped around for Odysseus and his gang in Greek mythology.

Yet for two thousand years, those in the vanguard of creating culture have often been magnetically drawn back to Jesus and the questions he poses to humanity concerning who he is (exploring themes of transcendence and immanence) and what he has done (themes of sacrifice, forgiveness and victory). In every cultural manifestation, there's always a point of contact with the true Christ for us to use to lovingly point others to him. Jesus Christ is relevant—yesterday, today and for ever.

Second, "Christ alone" should act as a sobering reminder of our call to holiness. In 1 Peter 1 v 17-19, the apostle says that we are to live in "reverent fear" for we know that "it was not with perishable things such as silver or gold that you were redeemed from the empty way of life handed down to you from your ancestors, but with the precious blood of Christ, a lamb without blemish or defect". We should be rightfully fearful of ever conducting ourselves in a way that suggests our new birth doesn't matter—

that Christ was wasting his time when he laid down his life and probably didn't need to bother. John Piper gives us a slap-around-the-face wake-up call here: "If we choose to endorse or embrace or enjoy or pursue impurity, we take a spear and ram it into Jesus's side every time we do. He suffered to set us free from impurity."[23]

Which leaves us with these questions as we consider "Can I watch?":

- In what way does this piece of culture communicate a longing for "something more"? What's the "point of contact" with Christ?

- Does my attitude towards this piece of culture reflect a "reverent fear" towards God? Would watching it lead me to endorse or embrace or enjoy or pursue impurity? What does that say about my attitude towards Christ?

## GOD'S GLORY ALONE

Finally, God's glory alone. This is the glue which sticks all the solas together and sums them all up: there's nothing we bring; it's all about him. Everything exists to display God's excellencies and to increase his fame. He glorifies himself in us and through us, his people. But we mustn't imagine him as an egocentric megalomaniac—the way God has wired us means that it's in living for his glory that we find our greatest joy and satisfaction. In previous chapters we've already thought about the cultural mandate, and our calling and vocation to take every thought captive for Christ. So whether God is being glorified or not is the ultimate litmus test of faithful cultural consumption and creation. Everything we do can be, and ought to be, done for his glory: "Whether you eat or drink or whatever you do, do it all for the glory of God" (1 Corinthians 10 v 31).

So our last question is a pretty simple one:

• Would watching _____ glorify God?

## FOUR GUIDES AND A REMINDER

So those are the questions we should be asking ourselves as we survey the vast offering on Netflix. But there are some practical guides that can help us faithfully consume culture too.

There's the internal check that we call our *conscience*. For Christians, this is our inner, God-given witness and warning system. Scripture says that we are always to obey it and should not go against it (Romans 14; 1 Corinthians 8). So, as a general rule, if watching something feels wrong, don't do it. Remember, too, that our freedom in Christ should not become a stumbling block for those whose conscience says differently. So even if you can watch something with a clear conscience, don't start raving about it in front of a Christian whose conscience might be grieved by it! "We who are strong ought to bear with the failings of the weak and not to please ourselves. Each of us should please our neighbours for their good, to build them up" (Romans 15 v 1-2). Importantly, our conscience certainly is not an infallible guide. It can be overly sensitive. It can go rogue and be seared (1 Timothy 4 v 2; Hebrews 10 v 22).

But our conscience can be a help, especially when it is cared for, trained, and calibrated by the truth.[24]

There's the external check of Christian *community*—Christians who know us really well and with whom there can be mutual honesty and accountability. How about watching shows communally rather than individually? This gives the opportunity to call things out and have conversations before and afterwards (and even during, if necessary). Again, community is not a magic bullet—if we can deceive ourselves, we can certainly deceive others—but it can definitely help.

Then there is the body of Christ, the *church*. Remember, our weekly gatherings are not a "holy huddle". They're more like an army medical tent that people are sent *to* from the battlefield before being sent *out* back into it. It's where we have our x-ray vision goggles polished. We're reminded of what God says is really important and praiseworthy, thrilled afresh by the Bible's story, and equipped to treasure Christ and live for him in the wider world.

Next, to keep the alliteration nice and neat, there's *circumvention*—ways to evade and bypass obstacles that would not be good for us to encounter:

- The hand over the eyes

- The hand on the fast-forward button

- The hand in the technology e.g. filtering services like VidAngel, which are more and more sophisticated

Again, these do not offer foolproof protection, and there comes a point where, if I'm spending most of my time looking at my hand, watching things at x30 normal speed, or watching disjointed clips because so much has been filtered out, then, quite frankly, what's the point?

Finally, remember that if we decide we should not watch something, we are not completely disqualified from commenting on it as we try to engage non-Christian friends with the gospel through it. We can still read about it and around it. In fact, our direct *disengagement* could be a countercultural witness which engages people with the gospel.

## TAKE A CULTURAL HEALTHCHECK

As we finish this chapter, here's a challenge. This week take an hour by yourself, or with those closest to you, and prayerfully do a health check of your cultural consumption and cultural creation. Put your listening, viewing and doing through our "five solas" test and discern the health of your heart. Is it functioning well? Does it need more exercise? Is it clogged up and so needs some interventions? The "only option" might give you a new lease of cultural life with which you can bless others and engage them with the truth. We'll find out how in the next chapter.

# 5. CONFRONT AND CONNECT: THE THEORY

*"I love it when a plan comes together"*
Hannibal, The A-Team

We have covered a lot of ground since Miley Cyrus opened the show. It's about time we took stock and started to put things together. We've been laying the groundwork of why Christians have to care about engaging with culture, what culture is and how culture works. In the last chapter we considered how, as disciples, we get our hearts in the right place as we consume and create culture. In the next couple of chapters we'll lay out a plan of practical "how to" ways we can engage with culture. Remember, as followers and ambassadors of the Lord Jesus, we want this engagement to result in us loving him more and more, and telling others to follow him with more and more clarity and persuasive power.

So pack your bags and put on the suncream. It's time for a Greek road trip.

## DESTINATION: CORINTH

Corinth in the first century: a bustling city of commerce and multiculturalism. Within its streets you'll find several temples to Greek deities, a Jewish synagogue and, more recently, a fledgling community of Christian believers. It is to this young church that the apostle Paul writes:

> [18] For the message of the cross is foolishness to those who are perishing, but to us who are being saved it is the power of God. [19] For it is written:
>
> "I will destroy the wisdom of the wise;
>   the intelligence of the intelligent I will frustrate."
>
> [20] Where is the wise person? Where is the teacher of the law? Where is the philosopher of this age? Has not God made foolish the wisdom of the world? [21] For since in the wisdom of God the world through its wisdom did not know him, God was pleased through the foolishness of what was preached to save those who believe. [22] Jews demand signs and Greeks look for wisdom, [23] but we preach Christ crucified: a stumbling-block to Jews and foolishness to Gentiles, [24] but to those whom God has called, both Jews and Greeks, Christ the power of God and the wisdom of God. [25] For the foolishness of God is wiser than human wisdom, and the weakness of God is stronger than human strength.          (1 Corinthians 1 v 18-25)

## THE GOSPEL THAT CONFRONTS

A few years ago I travelled to Manchester to take part in the BBC Radio 4 programme *Beyond Belief*, hosted by Ernie

Rea. The topic for discussion was "hell". As I've written on this area over the years, I sometimes get invited to speak about it in my capacity as "that weird guy who holds to a traditional belief in hell". With me on the panel that day were a liberal university theology lecturer and a Catholic journalist. Suffice it to say, they did not hold to a biblical view of hell in any orthodox way, and as the discussion progressed, we strongly disagreed.

What has stayed with me about that day was not that my fellow panellists found the thought of God punishing sins barbaric—although they did. Nor that they were offended by the justice of God—although they were. No, what struck me most was that their biggest snort of scepticism came when I spoke about the grace of God: "What, you're telling me that someone could live a terrible life but could confess their sins, be forgiven by Jesus and not go to hell?!" They thought both justice and grace were preposterous and laughable.

Yet the meeting of God's wrath—his right, justified anger at sin—and God's mercy—his total, undeserved forgiveness of sin—is at the heart of the Christian message. Right throughout the Bible these two truths are held in tension. They are two realities that seem impossible to reconcile—until, that is, Jesus Christ is crucified. On that day in history, God's wrath was poured out on his Son so that he can extend mercy to us. Now trusting in Christ's death and resurrection is the way to be saved—the *only* way to be saved.

But this sounds very strange to the world around us: "For the message of the cross is foolishness to those who are perishing, but to us who are being saved it is the power of God" (v 18).

Why does the message of the cross sound so foolish? Because, as 1 Corinthians 1 v 18-25 tells us, the gospel of Jesus Christ confronts *every* culture. There is nowhere in the world you can go where this won't sound odd. The idea of a Saviour who dies on a wooden cross reserved for criminals is a big fat contradiction to the world's way of doing things. We certainly wouldn't have written the story this way. It's utter foolishness. It's scandalous. It's deeply offensive. But it's through this message that God is pleased to "save those who believe" it (v 21).

The countercultural strangeness of this message means that sharing it with "those who are perishing" will always be hard. When it comes to our evangelism, there is, in the words of the evangelist Rico Tice, a "pain line" that we have to cross. There will always be an element of confrontation—a clash between a nonbeliever's way of seeing the world and God's way of seeing the world. We need the Holy Spirit to help us resist the temptation to avoid that confrontation by watering down the message or chopping off the unfashionable bits. We are not to be ashamed of God and the gospel.

And when it comes to our own discipleship, we're equally tempted to change what Jesus requires of his followers so that our lives can look more like those of the non-Christians around us—to make our values look more like the world's. Sadly, we know that there are many examples of those who do succumb to this temptation. We must be constantly praying that we do not.

## THE GOSPEL THAT CONNECTS

However, there are some Christians who don't mind the confrontation. They welcome the offence. So they'll preach a one-size-fits-all-sinners message no matter who's sitting in front of them. "After all, does it really matter?" this person might think. "The gospel's the gospel, right?" To do anything else would complicate things. Or worse, to adapt the message of Christ crucified to our audience might compromise the gospel, taking away its power. It's not that helpful to talk about the gospel being plausible or attractive, because the gospel is an offence.

But I don't think Paul thought like that. Instead, he makes the point of singling out two groups of people with two distinct cultures: "Jews demand signs and Greeks look for wisdom" (v 22).

There are the Jews—their worldview revolves around the idea of power. They grew up hearing the Old Testament stories of God's mighty power and miraculous signs: walking through the Red Sea between two walls of water; the walls of Jericho crashing down; wealthy kings like Solomon, to whom royalty from around the world came to pay homage. Power is what's important.

Then there are the Greeks—their culture places a premium on wisdom. Their history was filled with brilliant thinkers like Socrates, Plato and Aristotle. It's all about debate, rational arguments, rhetoric, philosophy, knowledge. Wisdom is what's important.

Jews don't look for wisdom and Greeks don't look for power. They have very different cultures and are captivated by different stories. And yet, if in our evangelism it doesn't matter who the audience is—if cultural context is totally irrelevant—then why does Paul distinguish between them?

Well, maybe Paul distinguishes these groups merely to highlight the massive contrast between Christ and every culture. Whether you're looking for power or for wisdom, Christ crucified is something totally and utterly different. He's "a stumbling-block to Jews and foolishness to Gentiles" (v 23). Christ confronts every culture.

Except then, in the next verse, Paul says something fascinating: "But to those whom God has called, both Jews and Greeks, Christ [is] the power of God and the wisdom of God" (v 24).

Jews have something they are looking for, and now Paul is saying that Jesus is that something. Greeks have something they are looking for, and Paul is saying that Jesus is that something too. Is this accommodating the message of Christ crucified to their specific cultures? Is this pandering to the cultural desires of Jews and Greeks? Is this Paul weakening the gospel's power?

*Not at all.* Rather, it's Paul *connecting* Christ crucified to the culture in front of him. He certainly preaches Christ crucified. He certainly says that Christ crucified is a "stumbling-block" and "foolishness". The message of the cross always *confronts* culture. But the message of the cross always *connects* too. Certainly, the power and wisdom of God in the crucified Christ is the opposite of the power and wisdom that Jews and Greeks expect. And yet, Christ crucified can be understood both in terms of power and wisdom—which makes a connection with

Jewish and Greek culture. Jewish Christians *and* Greek Christians can both look at the cross and see something which resonates deeply with their cultural background.

How is this possible?

Now I'm really hoping that as you're reading, this might be a "eureka" moment. That bit in the film where the protagonist gets a series of flashbacks in which everything is pieced together and starts to make sense.

Well, here come the flashbacks. Think about what we've said in our previous chapters about what culture is and how culture works.

- Think about human beings as culture-builders whose cultural products reflect their heart worship: either worship of God or worship of idols.

- Think about the connection between the "root" of our hearts and the "fruit" of the culture we create.

- Think about the nature of idolatry, which takes a good thing in creation and makes it into a god-thing.

- Think about the connection between the idolatrous counterfeit and the genuine original. Remember how our idols are always parasites on the truth and glimmer with elements of truth.

- Think about God messaging us in creation: how he gives a particular meaning to our reality and reveals his story of where this world is heading.

- Think about our sinful response: how we suppress God's story and substitute for it false stories which are twisted and distorted caricatures of the original.

Are the flashbacks making any sense yet? Can you see how the gospel connects? One helpful way of summarising this relationship between the gospel of Jesus and culture is the term "subversive fulfilment". The gospel is the subversive fulfilment of culture. This sounds a bit fancy and complicated but really it's not. It's describing how compared to the idolatrous stories that the world tells, the gospel both subverts and fulfils, confronts and connects.

It *subverts* in that it *confronts*, unpicks and overthrows the world's stories. It calls for new ways of looking at the world because the old ways are so useless and harmful. It's an appeal for repentance and faith in the better story of Christ crucified.

However, the gospel *fulfils* in that it *connects* and is shown to be worthy of our hopes and desires. The gospel is appealing in that it's a call to exchange old hopes and desires for new ones, *because these new ones are the originals from which our false stories are smudged and ripped fakes*.

So in the idolatrous cultural story of Jews and Greeks, "wisdom" and "power" are made to be the baddies. And yet when these things are reclaimed by Jesus and put into his true story, then they serve a glorious purpose. They are transformed and become ways to understand the meaning of Christ crucified. This is what this passage in 1 Corinthians tells us.

We need to think of the stories our culture tells us and the themes it peddles. Jews look for power; Greeks look for wisdom; your average 21st-century Westerner looks for...? Freedom? Peace? Satisfaction? Status? Identity? What is it that *you're* looking for? How does the gospel both confront and connect? How does the Christ crucified subversively fulfil these stories?

We need to be honest with ourselves. Some of us come from church backgrounds that are prone to stress the confrontation of Christ crucified. Or perhaps we were born with characters that are more direct. We worry less about the connection. Some of us come from church backgrounds or have characters that are prone to stress the connection aspect rather than the confrontation.

Paul says we are to do both *at the same time*. This is a hard balance to strike. So in the next few chapters, we are going to look at some examples of how we might read culture through a subversive fulfilment lens.

But before we do that, wouldn't it be awesome if we could not only see the theory of confronting and connecting but also see an example of Paul walking the talk?

Get back in the car; we're going to Athens.

# 6. CONFRONT
# AND CONNECT:
# IN PRACTICE

In the last five years, I've had the privilege of taking some of my kids to visit missionary friends in Athens. Without fail, our hosts always ask which places we'd especially like to go to—and without fail, my immediate response is the Areopagus, scene of one of Paul's most famous sermons, recorded in the book of Acts (Acts 17). Even though my kids groan at yet another trip there, I just don't care. It's become my own personal place of pilgrimage.

Of course, you have to use your imagination when visiting it today. It's nothing more than a huge hunk of uneven, black, shiny rock to clamber up on and walk around, being careful that the kids don't topple off the sheer drop at the back! (Greek culture seems to have a slightly different take on health and safety.) But when I'm there, I always like making the point, to anyone around who'll listen, that I'm actually standing on the place where the *actual* apostle Paul preached his *actual* sermon all that time ago. Just the historical "realness" of it all is so exhilarating. It's like a shot of apologetic adrenaline.

Paul's sermon to the Areopagus in Athens (which we'll get to in just a moment) shows us what "subversive fulfilment" looks like in practice. It's a "worked example" which takes our theory out of the classroom and into the messiness of real life with all its twists and turns—real life with all its unpredictability, where we need wisdom to know when and how to act and react to what's in front of us. Acts 17 is a textbook example of how cultural engagement can never be out of a textbook. It shows us how cultural engagement affects our head, our hands and our hearts.

And so I am thankful. Not only did this event really happen in space and time, but as a wonderful gift, the living God of the Bible got the 1st-century historian Doctor Luke to record it *then*, so that it would help me *now*. Isn't Scripture great?! When my own internal compass on life, the universe and everything is crazily spinning around, and I'm feeling dizzy and, frankly, quite travel-sick, I know that my loving heavenly Father has given me an infallible guide so I can re-orientate myself with confidence in my 21st-century surroundings.

## PAUL'S ATTITUDE AND OURS

Well into his second missionary journey, a solitary Paul is on a stop-over in Athens, having sent his friends off to collect Silas and Timothy, who were still in Berea. One can imagine him, like any tourist with time to kill, wandering around this proud city renowned for its history, learning and cultural creations. However, in verse 16 our focus is entirely drawn to the fact that Paul "was greatly distressed to see that the city was full of idols". At several points in the Old Testament, we see that God was provoked by idols (for example, in Deuteronomy 32 v 16-19), because they detract from his own glory—the glory that is rightfully his. Now for God's sake, Paul is similarly provoked as he surveys the scene in front of him. It is this reaction which gives us the mood music for the whole Athenian encounter. However respectful and engaging Paul may be in what follows, we must not forget his attitude to the scene before him. It's confrontation.

This presents us with two challenges. First, in our "politically correct", "tolerant", "multicultural" context, are we going to have the biblical eyes—and, frankly, the biblical nerve—to see and feel all cultural encounters in the context of idolatry? Are we going to be suitably provoked by that? I'm not talking about red-faced ranting and raving, but a serious, settled, deep-seated commitment which understands the real, sinister nature of all that which sets itself up as a rival to God—however it might look to the contrary on the surface. As we look across our communities and our nation, do we have that passion for God's glory? Are we grieved that idolatry tramples all over it? Or have we become desensitised? Should we be more distressed than we often are? Would there be a renewed urgency to our mission if we shared Paul's attitude?

Second, Paul's distress leads to a determination and drive to proclaim the truth and to work hard at communication. The next verse tells us, "So he reasoned in the synagogue with both Jews and God-fearing Greeks, as well as in the market-place day by day with those who happened to be there". Paul is not content to wash his hands of Athens and its inhabitants, leaving them stuck in their idolatry. Instead he gets straight into strategic and thought-through evangelism. We know enough about Paul, his life and his gospel to be sure that his motivation is not fuelled by malice or pride but by a deep compassion and love for those who are lost because they do not know the Lord Jesus Christ. Paul himself was a living testimony of someone who had been lost and distant from God, but who had been wonderfully and graciously "found" by the risen Lord Jesus Christ.

Paul knew a better story than those of idols—the *best* story of the good news of the gospel. I know it's a cliché, but gospel proclamation really is one beggar telling another beggar where to find bread. Or more biblically, it's about finding thirsty people who are on their hands and knees trying to lick up stagnant residue from a broken pot, getting them to "stop and think", and turning them to find a stream of living water (Jeremiah 2 v 13; Isaiah 44 v 19).

We're to have a passion for God's glory and a passion for lost souls. We're to be distressed over idolatry and distressed for those who worship them. And this must lead us to speak up in confronting and connecting with culture.

## PAUL'S APPROACH AND OURS

Paul's reasoning in the synagogue and market-place catches the attention of some of Athens' finest philosophers, who invite him to speak at the Areopagus—

the Supreme Court of sorts—to explain himself. And what does Paul say?

Well, it's not quite what we perhaps expect to find. It's not the sort of full-on, step-by-step gospel presentation that we might have come across in our favourite evangelistic tract. He doesn't seem to cover all the bases. But this is not a problem or deficiency. Why? Because he's already been proclaiming "the good news of Jesus and his resurrection" before being brought before the Areopagus (Acts 17 v 18). Paul is certainly preaching Christ crucified.

But the reaction to this message is one of confusion. The philosophers who hear him in the market-place literally call him a "seed-picker" (v 18): one who scavenges and pecks at various ideas without really understanding any of them. Therefore, when Paul stands up and starts to speak in front of the council, his purpose is to give a defence of this good news—to put it in the context of life, the universe and everything:

> Paul then stood up in the meeting of the Areopagus
> and said: "People of Athens! I see that in every
> way you are very religious. For as I walked around
> and looked carefully at your objects of worship, I
> even found an altar with this inscription: TO AN
> UNKNOWN GOD. So you are ignorant of the very
> thing you worship—and this is what I am going to
> proclaim to you."                    (Acts 17 v 22-23)

If this isn't subversive fulfilment, then I don't know what is! Paul has spent time carefully looking at the culture around him, looking for ways in—that chink in the armour that he can exploit. He's listening. He's watching. He's connecting. He sees that the Athenians are very religious. So much so that they don't want to risk leaving any gods out—they've got an altar "to an unknown god" to cover their backs just in case. So Paul appeals to their apparent open-mindedness. He connects with their culture's desire to know the divine and worship appropriately.

And yet this contact is not a warm handshake affirming them in their religiosity. He's not affirming them in their idolatry. Rather, it's more like the contact of a rugby scrum: he calls them ignorant! He's confronting.

Connecting, confronting: subversive fulfilment.

Let's start thinking then. When it comes to our secular culture, what are the "unknown gods"? Where can they be found? How are those who are seemingly uninterested in Christianity actually very religious? What's our way in?

Next, we come to Paul's speech itself:

The God who made the world and everything in it is the Lord of heaven and earth and does not live in temples built by human hands. And he is not served by human hands, as if he needed anything. Rather, he himself gives everyone life and breath and everything else. From one man he made all the nations, that they should inhabit the whole earth; and he marked out their appointed times in history and the boundaries of their lands. God did this so that they would seek him and perhaps reach out for him and find him, though he is not far from any one of us. "For in him we live and move and have our being." As some of your own poets have said, "We are his offspring."

Therefore since we are God's offspring, we should not think that the divine being is like gold or silver or stone—an image made by human design and skill. In the past God overlooked such ignorance, but now he commands all people everywhere to repent. For he has set a day when he will judge the world with justice by the man he has appointed. He has given proof of this to everyone by raising him from the dead.

(17 v 24-31)

What Paul is doing here is giving a *run-up* and then a *run-through*. For the good news of Jesus to make sense in Athens, Paul needs the longer run-up, which connects with what the Athenians *do* know and fills in the gaps. He gets some basic stuff in place—stuff which the Athenians just don't have. And then he jumps off into a run-through of a Christian way of viewing the world. Paul is saying, *OK, let's get back to basics. You Athenians may have all kinds of views about the nature of ultimate reality, creation, time, the end of it all, but I'm going to lay out how I see it.* And here's the crucial point: without these basic building blocks in place, Jesus and his resurrection do not make sense.

So here are our next set of challenges for our evangelism. In our increasingly "post-Christian", biblically illiterate culture, we need to be starting further back with those who aren't Christians. We need to spend more time going through these basics, putting together a picture into which Jesus and his resurrection make sense. We need to deal with those cultural "blocks" and "bouncers" which get in the way of people giving the good news a hearing.

Please don't mishear me at this point: our goal is always to present people with Jesus. This running up and running through is not a *substitute* for gospel proclamation, but rather, a *support* for such proclamation. And it will take more time and patience and prayer than maybe we've needed in the past.

Here's one example of how we can do this: when people tell me they don't believe in God, I often say, "I bet I don't believe in the God you don't believe in". It's essential that we distinguish the living God of the Bible from what other people *think* God is like. And so, as we speak and listen, we need to make sure that we are clearing the ground by dealing with the misunderstandings that people have. "Look, I know what you think about who God is, but from now on when I talk about 'God' I mean this…"

And what do we mean? Well, we should look no further than Paul's own outline in verses 24-31, in which he lays out the fundamentals of a Christian view of the world. This is a super-charged, super-condensed statement of theology, steeped in the Old Testament. Paul describes the Creator God, who has made everything, sustains everything and is sovereign over everything, and who is in no way dependent on this creation. But at the same time, he is a personal God who can be spoken of in personal terms and who engages with his creation personally. Therefore, he's a God who is not so far off that we can't know him, but nor is he so near that he is indistinguishable from his creation.

Moreover, Paul describes a linear view of human history, which can talk about both origins and endings. He hints at an understanding of providence which has a purpose; at something that's gone horribly wrong so that we are left "groping after" the truth; and at a time during which God is patient, but also at an end to history with a judgment coming.

Just in this little summary, do you realise how many other worldviews we have knocked out? Here's the challenge: do you know these fundamental building blocks deeply enough to be able to communicate them simply? This isn't something just for other more intelligent or more gifted Christians. It's for every Christian. If we want to proclaim Jesus and the resurrection, we can't help but get theological.

## PAUL'S APPEAL AND OURS

Paul's speech comes to a crescendo with this impassioned appeal:

> [30] In the past God overlooked such ignorance, but now he commands all people everywhere to repent. [31] For he has set a day when he will judge the world with justice by the man he has appointed. He has given proof of this to everyone by raising him from the dead. (17 v 30-31)

There are two things to note here. First, when we think of the resurrection, we often tend to think of new life, new beginnings, hope and joy. These are all wonderfully true of course. But that is not how the resurrection is used by

Paul in verse 31. Here the resurrection of Jesus Christ is the proof that a just judgment is coming. The resurrection is the greatest public proclamation to the whole world that Jesus Christ has been vindicated and given all authority. He is both just Judge and Saviour Lord. This truth ought to form an integral part of our gospel presentations, no matter what "sneering" may ensue (v 32).

Second, Paul is not shy about calling for repentance (v 30). Idols are not a "stepping stone" on the way to Jesus. Christianity is not an extra that you can tack onto your existing lifestyle. Repentance is a 180-degree turn from idolatry to Jesus.

So here are our last challenges: in our sentimental, "progressive" culture, we must not forget to talk about judgment, together with the command (yes, command) for *repentance* and faith. Such a call, of course, is countercultural—but not as unpersuasive as we sometimes think. Yes, in our cultural context there is an ongoing and sometimes legitimate suspicion of authority, which means that when it comes to God, many people imagine him as a divine dictator. And yet, as beings created for worship, we are all under authorities all the time. As one of our own poets (Bob Dylan) so eloquently put it, "You're gonna have to serve somebody".

Jesus Christ is the Servant King who has both the might and the right to rule his creation. For those who bow the knee, his yoke is easy and his burden light. Obedience and love are a happy marriage. Moreover, the idea that every human being is accountable for their actions and that there will be a judgment in which all wrongs will be righted is actually attractive, and so much more attractive than "imagining" a world where "above us" there is "only sky". That history is heading somewhere and means something does resonate with us deep down.

However, we must not forget the urgency of all this. There is a warning here. *Now* is the time to turn, before it is too late. God's incredible tolerance and patience, which we live under now, will one day come to end. That big canvas is going to break. As Paul indicates elsewhere, to not turn from idols to serve the living and true God will mean no rescue from the coming wrath (1 Thessalonians 1 v 9b-10). As with all creaturely rebellion against the Creator, sin is bad, mad and deeply sad. So however painful and uncomfortable we find it, to fail to communicate this warning is most unloving.

When we do appeal to people to repent, then, like Paul, we can expect a mixed response:

> [32] When they heard about the resurrection of the dead, some of them sneered, but others said, "We want to hear you again on this subject." [33] At that, Paul left the Council. [34] Some of the people became followers of Paul and believed. Among them was Dionysius, a member of the Areopagus, also a woman named Damaris, and a number of others.
>
> (17 v 32-34)

When we connect and confront culture with the gospel, however lovingly we do it, some people will "sneer"— they'll think we're stupid, or bigoted, or both. And that's OK—that's normal. Others will have had their interest piqued and will be open to hearing more another time. That's why evangelism is usually best done in the context of ongoing personal relationships, and we need to be ready to talk about Jesus more than once with people. At the same time, we don't need to treat our flatmates to a full-blown Bible exposition after every episode of *The Crown*. Sometimes a "little and often" approach is more appropriate.

But don't set your expectations too low. If we prayerfully and faithfully share the gospel with lots of people—connecting with and confronting their worldview with the good news of Jesus—we can expect some people to respond in belief. And sometimes, as with Dionysius in verse 34, it's the people we'd least expect.

# 7. YOUR TURN: CULTURAL ENGAGEMENT FOR DISCIPLES

I know what you're thinking. You've read about Paul confronting and connecting in Athens. You're sort of encouraged that we have a practical example and model of cultural engagement in the Bible. But here's the big discouragement: you're no apostle Paul. You don't have his background, his training or his calling. You don't have his passion for God's glory. You're in no way as godly. How could you ever engage in the way he does?

What's more, his context and yours are worlds apart. You're not an itinerant missionary, going from city to city—cutting-edge cultural centres of power and influence—to explain the gospel to the great and good. Your week has revolved around getting through work, struggling to decide what's for dinner each evening, and collapsing in front of the TV after putting the kids to bed. You don't have the time or energy to be at the forefront of a cultural revolution. What difference can you make?

Now that you've read as far as chapter 7, I need to let you into a little secret. For someone whose job it is to teach Christians about theology, culture and apologetics, when it comes to my own cultural diet I am, quite frankly, something of a disappointment. Unlike some academics I know, I don't have a blog, a vlog, or a podcast. I don't tweet. I've got Netflix and have a few shows I watch, but I can't say I binge-watch when I get behind. In fact, although this is apparently the golden age of the small screen, I just feel harangued when I'm told about all the stuff I have to be watching (and the blogs I have to be reading about the shows I have to be watching). I love music, but my tastes aren't particularly "on trend"—in fact, they are rather old-fashioned and niche for a guy in his 40s (late 20th-century Russian pianist Sviatoslav Richter, anyone?).

Our family tradition of watching West Ham United play football is often an experience of existential angst, and not simply because of our team's poor performance—invariably at some point in every game, I find myself surveying in slow-motion the baying crowd of 57,000 people around me, and with a heavy heart I recognise how overwhelmed and incompetent I feel in trying to connect with and confront your average 21st-century secular Brit with the gospel.

Cultural analysis doesn't come easily to me—I'm as bewitched, bothered and bewildered as the rest of us. I am certainly no apostle Paul. So if you've read this far and don't feel up to the task, you're not the only one. But don't despair and give up, because this stuff matters—if you care about Jesus, then you care about following Jesus, and you care about telling others about Jesus. If you're human, you are a cultural creature. So with whatever gifts God has given us and in whatever context he has placed us, we are called to be faithful to this calling.

Moreover, I'm also a parent of children aged from twenty down to four, and a church elder at a multicultural inter-generational church. It's crucial I try to get a grasp of what those under my parental and pastoral care are into so I can care for them properly. My passion as a theologian has always been to think theologically about culture in general, and our culture in particular, and always with a view to training ordinary people to think theologically about culture.

You and I are not the apostle Paul. Yet in the pages of Scripture, our gracious heavenly Father has given us models like Paul, who give us a pattern to help us engage faithfully and fruitfully. That's what the rest of this chapter is about—it's a "how to" chapter, not for professional elites but for beginners. We're not learning how to run a marathon. We're more like those training to run a 5K—starting small but little by little getting stronger and stronger.

This is cultural engagement not for dummies but for disciples.

## THE "SUBVERSIVE FULFILMENT" APPROACH

If we go back to Paul's subversive fulfilment approach in Acts 17, we can discern four steps to cultural engagement.

1. *Entering:* Stepping into the world and listening to the story: "For as I walked around and looked carefully at your objects of worship..." (v 23)

2. *Exploring:* Searching for elements of grace and the idols attached to them: "People of Athens! I see that in every way you are very religious. For as I walked around and looked carefully at your objects of worship, I even found an altar with this inscription: TO AN UNKNOWN GOD." (v 23)

3. *Exposing*: Showing up the idols as destructive frauds: "Therefore since we are God's offspring, we should not think that the divine being is like gold or silver or stone—an image made by human design and skill." (v 29)

4. *Evangelising*: Showing off the gospel of Jesus Christ as "subversive fulfilment": "So you are ignorant of the very thing you worship—and this is what I am going to proclaim to you." (v 23)

We go about doing this "subversive fulfilling" in many different ways. We do it through communication: that could be an informal ongoing conversation with a non-Christian family member, a one-off comment to a stranger on the train, a one-to-one discipleship session over a coffee, the chat you have with a group of mates after a film or a match, a sermon given by a pastor to his congregation, or a piece in a church magazine.

But we also do subversive fulfilling through community: we engage with a particular culture not just in the words we speak but in our practices, our daily routines and our weekly rituals. It's about our ways-of-being-together—in our families, in our churches as we gather together week by week, and as we are scattered into the world in all our callings and vocations. It's about how we model cross-shaped love, inclusion, tolerance and freedom in our hospitality around the kitchen table and around the communion table.

Before we go any further I have a *big* disclaimer. I'm describing these steps as a "pattern" or "approach" of cultural engagement. I choose these words very deliberately. What I am describing is definitely not a formula or a technique. It's not a magic bullet, a "one size fits all", "slot tab A into opening B" process or mechanism. Why? Because our engagement gets complicated and messy as we interact with flesh-and-blood people in all their wonderful and frustrating predictability and unpredictability.

So, we need to be flexible. These four steps give us a shape to our engagement, but there is also freedom to mix it up. We need to be both proactive and reactive—deliberately intentional and able to spontaneously improvise. This flexibility also means that while there is a kind of order to the steps, it's not always clear cut. For example, notice in Acts 17 that before Paul's address to the Areopagus, he was already "preaching the good news about Jesus and the resurrection" (verse 18). What I have put as the last step actually comes first in Athens! However, when Paul is speaking at the Areopagus, the "reveal" of Jesus, the resurrection and the need for repentance (the evangelism bit) comes as the climax of a careful argument which starts with entry, exploration and exposing.

Let's break down these stages into a little more detail.

## 1. ENTER: STEPPING INTO THE WORLD AND LISTENING TO THE STORY

First, we step into the culture we are engaging with. Crucially, we need to do something that many of us are not very good at in our relationships: we need to listen. "Entering" is about patient observing, watching and listening. It's about careful description without jumping to conclusions or caricaturing. It's about being empathetic, asking lots of questions and gathering lots of information. If we are going to confront and connect, we need to know precisely what we are confronting and connecting with. We need to be on "receive" mode, describing what's there without prescribing what we think should or shouldn't be there. At this stage we need to try and be charitable.

It can be helpful to ask some basic questions of the cultural "text" or artefact. It's worth saying that in this chapter, when I talk about "texts", this doesn't always mean something written down. A film, TV commercial, video game, interior-design trend or dance craze is just as much of a "text" as a book or a blog post. Depending on the text you're trying to engage with, not all the questions will be relevant. Just run with the ones that are.

   a. *What does it say?* What's the story and the mood? Use all five senses here—what does it look like, sound like, feel like, taste like, even smell like?
   b. *Who wrote it?* What's the context of the artefact you are looking at? Do some digging. Get behind the scenes and look at the history. What do we know about the creator(s) of this text?

c. *Who reads it?* Who is the audience and how are they being affected? Use your imagination. What would the world look like if this cultural text had its way? What would we be like? What's the impact and influence of the text—have people bought into it or not?

Now, it can get a little complicated because a feedback loop emerges between the text, its creators, and its audience. Just think of how Hollywood film producers might make changes to a final scene after audience reactions to a pre-release screen test, or the decision to make or not to make a sequel based on ticket sales. What this shows us is that culture is always evolving and moving on.

At this point, and having done this analysis, you might be able to have a shot at suggesting the false gospel story this text is telling. How does it answer questions like: Who are we as human beings? What's our place in the universe? What's gone wrong? What's the solution? What happens when we die?

## 2. EXPLORE: SEARCHING FOR ELEMENTS OF GRACE AND THE IDOLS ATTACHED TO THEM

Our second step is about starting to see the world with our theological x-ray goggles on. Having listened carefully and charitably, we can afford to be a little more suspicious at this stage as we flash back to our flashback in chapter 5:

• Think about human beings as culture-builders whose cultural products reflect their heart worship: either worship of God or worship of idols.

- Think about the connection between the "root" of our hearts and the "fruit" of the culture we create.

- Think about the nature of idols and idolatry, which takes a good thing in creation and makes it into a god-thing.

- Think about the connection between the idolatrous counterfeit and the genuine original. Remember how our idols are always parasites on the truth and glimmer with elements of truth.

- Think about God messaging us in creation: how he gives a particular meaning to our reality and reveals his story of where this world is heading.

- Think about our sinful response: how we suppress God's story and substitute for it false stories which are twisted and distorted caricatures of the original.

This allows us to ask questions like these:

d. How is the text interpreting and reinterpreting God's messages of shadows and sunbeams?
e. What's true, good, helpful and beautiful about it? And how is this being suppressed and distorted in an unhelpful and destructive way?
f. Is the text positively amplifying God's messages and leading us back to him? Or is it negatively suppressing, muting and graffiti-ing over God's messages, and so leading us to an idol that humans have created?

## 3. EXPOSE: SHOWING UP THE IDOLS AS DESTRUCTIVE FRAUDS

Our third step is the difficult one: getting people to "stop and think" about the cultural stories told by our texts (Isaiah 44 v 19). These are stories that our friends are enchanted by, but that are slowly killing them as they drink from those cracked cisterns. How do we get them to sit up and listen?

This is where we have to do the theological equivalent of a Paddington Bear "hard stare". It's all about metaphorically pricking bubbles and pouring on cold water—trying to rouse people out of the living nightmare they are in. Again, we can do this by asking penetrating questions to try and show how these cultural artefacts can't deliver on what they promise—they are not true, or good or beautiful. Questions like:

- How is that working for you?

- I'm really interested to know—why does this seem so compelling to you?

- If you've got a moment, can I show you why that might not be the best way of looking at this?[25]

As my friend Ted Turnau says, we need to show up the "explanatory poverty" of people's idols: they may talk a good game but that's all they are—talk. At the end of the day, they have no real answers and can't even justify their good bits! And even good things made into ultimate things become idolatrous things.

## 4. EVANGELISE: SHOWING OFF THE GOSPEL OF JESUS CHRIST AS "SUBVERSIVE FULFILMENT"

Our final step should be the most satisfying, but in my experience it can be as painful as the previous step!

When we come to the evangelising bit, we probably know that it's going to mean saying something about Jesus. But given our cultural analysis and its context, exactly what and how are we going to communicate about Jesus?

What I'm not suggesting is an overly-spiritualised, cut-and-paste, repent-or-burn message that we've neatly packaged into some easily memorised sound-bite chunks. Instead we want to present a big-picture, new way of looking at the world, based on the life, death, resurrection and ascension of Jesus Christ. The gospel has something to say about anything and everything, because the gospel impacts anything and everything—both in the "not-yet" of eternity (in the realities of heaven and hell) and the "now" of our lives, families, communities and the church. Like Paul, we preach Christ crucified, yes—but always within a particular cultural story, answering particular questions, hopes, fears, dreams and desires: always confronting, always connecting.

Here's an example I've quoted before from a former student of mine:

I was recently asked to talk about faith to a group of professional sportsmen. I began by exploring the issue of identity and tried to highlight how their impression of themselves has been determined

by the opinion of others from a very early age ...
Teachers, coaches, age group coaches, professional
coaches, international coaches, media, fans...

In the eyes of these people their value is
determined by their performance, and I tried to get
them to see that tying their joy or satisfaction—
ultimately their identity—to these things is a
volatile thing that leaves them very vulnerable ...
One of the players said that he agreed with this and
that was why he didn't put "all his eggs in the sport
basket". His "faith" was his family. I then explored
how that too will ultimately leave you vulnerable ...

From there I held out Christ as the only certain
and sure place to stand, and the only place where
identity is secure. I said that as long as our family,
coaches, fans, [or the] media make their demands,
we will have to measure up; as such, we will lie and
put on a front when things are bad. Christ knows
the worst about us and accepts us anyway. The
opinions and love of others are fickle, changing
according to our performance. Christ accepts us
unconditionally, liberating us to be honest and
humble towards others ... Of course, I had to show
them how living with the focus on themselves as
the end of all things might be offensive to God ...
Finding security in Christ can only happen if you
repent of those things.

One guy asked me what he needs to do to become a
Christian, and now another wants to read a Gospel.

I'm 100% certain this wouldn't have happened if my presentation had been a standard "God's in charge, you have sinned, it's going to go badly, so you better repent" approach.[26]

## OVER TO YOU...

Now it's time for you to have a go. You might want to do this exercise yourself, or better still with a group of friends. You could make an evening of it! I hope this guided exercise through a particular cultural "text" will give you a boost of confidence and kick-start you into doing your own analysis on a whole range of topics.

Finding good cultural examples that resonate with everyone is tricky, indeed impossible. So if the one I've chosen doesn't resonate with you, feel free to substitute something else.

I'm writing this chapter in the aftermath of England being knocked out of the 2018 Football World Cup. For those living in England over the last few weeks, it has been a surreal experience and a "cultural moment" that has captured a nation's imagination. Football fever took over as England's young and inexperienced squad, managed by Gareth Southgate, exceeded expectations with a succession of victories which took them all the way through to the semi-finals for the first time since 1990 (we failed to even get out of the group stage in 2014).

At the centre of the nation's growing interest in the progress of the national football team was the slogan "It's coming home", uttered and memed literally hundreds of thousands of times. So we are going to focus on "It's coming home" as a way to describe and analyse a cultural moment that many of us lived through.

You'll work through the four stages we've covered in earlier in this chapter: Enter, Explore, Expose, Evangelise.

Let's be clear: I'm not going to do the work for you. But I will prompt you with some questions and give some hints which might help you in your analysis. You'll probably find that you'll need your brain, a pen, and access to a search engine.

As you do this general analysis, try to think of specifics too. For example, think of a friend or family member who was completely captivated by the experience. What would you say to them? How might you confront and connect with this story, and with them? If you watched the England games or read about them afterwards, think back to how you responded at the time. If you could go back in time, how might what you've read in this book have affected your evangelism to those around you?

When you've done this analysis, why not finish by praying through some of the things you've thought about?

My prayer is that you'll get a taste for this and want to do more. Once you've worked through this example, choose something else you are interested in. Choose something your friends and family are interested in. Have a go at working through the stages. Perhaps it could be the start of a regular cultural workshop? Perhaps you could invite your non-Christian friends to come and chat with you?

You won't find it easy at first—doing this cultural analysis is countercultural to us! But I hope and pray that as you get going and it becomes a habit, it will help you engage more faithfully and more fruitfully.

Just imagine a generation of disciples all over the country and all over the world engaging with culture for Christ and his glory. And then go for it!

## "IT'S COMING HOME"

But when one does find depth in popular culture, it is important to take note, for there the deep desires of the many coalesce. When one sees idolatry in popular culture, one catches a view of a society's widespread affliction and affection, of the tempting and terrible effects of the Fall played out culture-wide. When one sees grace, one catches a glimpse—if only for a brief moment—of that culture healed and cleansed, of God speaking his truth to the people, of popular culture the way it was meant to be. That is why I believe it important to listen to popular culture. In popular culture, we see popular desire laid bare. And it needs a Christian response.[27]

The slogan "It's coming home" comes from the song "Three Lions (Football's Coming Home)" by The Lightning Seeds and comedians Frank Skinner and David Baddiel. Originally released in 1996 to mark England hosting the European Championships, it reached number 1 in the UK singles charts again in 2018 during England's World Cup run. Start by looking up the lyrics and listening to the song or watching the music video on YouTube. The memorable refrain is:

It's coming home, it's coming home, it's coming,
Football's coming home.

## 1. ENTER: STEPPING INTO THE WORLD AND LISTENING TO THE STORY

### What does it say?

    a. Think of some of the main themes that are in the text and the World Cup experience as a whole. What's the story that's being told? How is it being told?

### Hints

In the middle of England's run, Gary Parkinson wrote a detailed analysis of the song in which he covered many angles historically, culturally and musically. Here are some excerpts from the beginning and end of his piece which might act as a prompt:

> Like so many pop songs, "Three Lions" is about love and loss, but it's also about cultural identity, about longing and belonging, about people and place, about nationhood and about the irretrievability of the past and the possibilities of the future. It keys into a very English trait of gently expecting disappointment: "Hanging on in quiet desperation is the English way," as Pink Floyd put it on "Dark Side of the Moon". It's not so much outright negativity as slight bewilderment that things have gone so far downhill from a previous position atop the global pile. Indeed, you could replace much

of the football content with similarly structured sentiments about a post-industrial malaise, the late-20th-century loss of historical national pride and achievement stretching back through world wars and the Victorian era to Waterloo, the Industrial Revolution and on back into history's mists. But of course, it's about football...

[The song is] a cultural touchstone. It's inclusive, not aggressive. It's not about war and fighting, it's about dreaming. It's frequently sung by drunkards in public but usually in an attempt to provoke a mass singalong rather than to prove their individuality or masculinity. Try singing it angrily; it just doesn't work. Anyone who tries is utterly missing the point.

As Broudie puts it: "It's a very emotional record that sidesteps all that horrible stuff, and goes right to the heart of when you're just a kid supporting a football team. At the most raw, emotional times, people sing together, whether it's a funeral or football match. 'Three Lions' has something of that—we're all in this together, we're all willing to dream."

"Three Lions" does that through a brilliant crystallisation of a certain sort of Englishness. It's about the near-parodical national trait of waiting patiently and queueing diligently while hoping fervently. It's about the possibility of greatness, but also of a unifying happiness and celebration. It's about empathy and community and love and hope and dreams. That's what makes us human, and that's what makes "Three Lions" so popular and perfect.[28]

You might also think of some of the words used in the discussion around the World Cup in terms of the slogan, the English team and Gareth Southgate in particular (for example, destiny, fate, redemption).

Some other contextual factors to consider: the heatwave the country was experiencing; Brexit discussions in turmoil with high-profile government resignations; imminent state visit of President Trump.

Some stats from *The Sun* newspaper:

[England's semi-final defeat to Croatia] was watched by 30.9 million people on ITV, surpassing the 30.15 million who watched the Den and Angie Watts divorce drama on EastEnders in 1986. Only the 1966 World Cup final and Princess Diana's funeral in 1997 were watched by more people, but they were both shown on BBC and ITV. The audience for the Croatia game was made up of 26.6 million watching on ITV and another 4.3 million who used its online service ITV Hub. More than 80 per cent of the nation's TV viewers watched the game, with an average of 24.3 million watching between kick-off and the final whistle. The true total could be even higher as it does not include those watching in public venues.[29]

### Who wrote it?

    b.  Who was behind the song? What do we know about them and their background?

### Who reads it?

    c.  Who was the audience for the song and how were they being affected? What would the world look like if this cultural text had its way? What would we be like? What's the impact and influence of the text? Did people buy into it or not?

    *Bonus question:* If I said to you that "Three Lions" was a hymn, or that the phrase "It's coming home" was a liturgy, how would you react?

### Hints

Here's a sample of media reaction to what was going in the days after the semi-final defeat:

> England had history in their hands and a first World Cup final since 1966 in their sights as the clock ticked past 10 p.m. in Moscow—only to let it all slip away and so leave this historic city with familiar feelings of despair and disappointment … The years of hurt will go on—and for all the optimism raised by England's deeds in Russia over the last month, there will be a burning sense of missed opportunity that will take a long time to erase. (Phil McNulty, BBC)

A tweet from the England camp the day after their defeat:

To everyone who supported us.
To everyone who believed this time was different.
To everyone who wasn't afraid to dream.
To everyone who knows this is only the beginning.
Thank you. We hope we made you proud.
#threelions

Writing in the *Irish Times*, Ken Early argues that "It's coming home" went from an ironic joke to arrogant prediction which gave the Croatian players motivation:

So "It's coming home" started out as a self-deprecating joke, rapidly engulfed the planet while mutating into something less self-deprecating, and ultimately helped to fuel the Croatian fury that knocked England out. In the end the only ones that weren't laughing were the English. It must seem today that they can't win no matter what they do, but at least this time they gave it a better-than-average go.

Ahead of the semi-final the New Identity Tattoo Studio made this announcement on Facebook: "To celebrate England getting to the semi-finals, we've decided to do FREE 'It's coming home' tattoos all this week."

The National Centre for Domestic Violence launched an "If England get beaten, so will she" campaign ahead of the World Cup semi-final. The campaign highlighted that domestic violence increases 26% when England play and 38% when England lose.

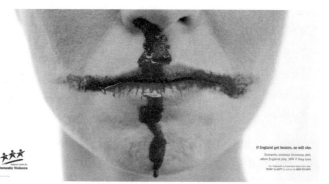

If England get beaten, so will she.

Domestic violence increases 26% when England play, 38% if they lose.

For help with a domestic injustice call 'NOW' to 60777 or call us on 0808 914 0292

National Centre for
Domestic Violence

## 2. EXPLORE: SEARCHING FOR ELEMENTS OF GRACE AND THE IDOLS ATTACHED TO THEM

    d. How is the "text" interpreting and reinterpreting God's messages of shadows and sunbeams?

    e. What's true, good, helpful and beautiful about it, in terms of God's common grace? How is this being suppressed and distorted in unhelpful and destructive ways?

    f. Is "It's coming home" amplifying God's messages and leading us back to him, or is it negatively suppressing, muting and graffiti-ing God messages, and so leading us to an idol that we have created?

### Hints

Some themes to consider: community, communal experience, home, belonging, identity, hope, Englishness and national identity.

## 3. EXPOSE: SHOWING UP THE IDOLS AS DESTRUCTIVE FRAUDS

g. How would you get people to "stop and think" about the story told by the text? How would you pour cold water on the dream? How would you point to the "explanatory poverty" of the text?

### Obvious hint

It didn't come home, did it? What was the aftermath of the defeat?

## 4. EVANGELISE: SHOWING OFF THE GOSPEL OF JESUS CHRIST AS "SUBVERSIVE FULFILMENT"

h. How does the gospel confront and connect with the text in a subversive-fulfilment way? Be concrete and specific.

### Hint

Here is a helpful little piece written by Jonny Ivey for website *Heirs Magazine* on July 7th, the day of the England quarter-final against Sweden:

> The English perception of ourselves is never clearer than during major football tournaments.
>
> The Lightning Seeds capture it well with their classic song ... Modern psychology would call it a self-esteem problem. We're pretty down on ourselves. Contrast this with our Australian or

American friends, who seem so confident. They're not "gonna throw it away". They're gonna win. But us? Maybe. But we'll probably blow it away.

An American once told me that British culture is humble. But we shouldn't confuse high or low self-esteem with pride and humility.

Self-esteem—whether high or low—is based on the self. On pride. It's about my ability or inability to live up to a standard.

And it's shaky. After England beat Colombia, suddenly the pundits moved on from the doldrums to the chorus—"Football's coming home!"

Self-esteem is based on our performance. BBC Sport illustrated this well with [an] Instagram photo of Gareth Southgate. Its title? "Redemption."

Self-esteem is a precarious ball-game. Our condemnation or redemption depends on our performance. On that penalty [which Southgate missed against Germany in 1996]. Our sense of self flip-flops like the Lightning Seeds song.

But not so our identity in Christ. God's grace levels the playing field. There are no winners and losers in the church. We're all losers, basking in the victory of Christ (Colossians 2 v 15). No one qualifies after good performance or gets eliminated due to poor performance. When we're obedient, we praise Jesus for that joy.

When we're disobedient, we repentantly praise Jesus that we're no less clothed with his perfect righteousness (2 Corinthians 5 v 21).

So tonight, whether England win or lose, redemption's secure. Your identity doesn't waiver. You can celebrate without being proud. Or be disappointed without being crushed.[30]

i. Finally, think about next steps. How might you have engaged some specific people you know on this subject? How might the conversation have gone? What would you have written on Facebook? What other means of communication might you have engaged through? How could you keep the conversation going?

Pray about the themes and people you've thought about in doing this analysis.

# HERE ARE SOME I PREPARED EARLIER...

And so this story about cultural engagement starts to come to an end. You've seen the rationale, the theology, the biblical examples, and even had a go yourself. I hope you're persuaded that you—yes, you—can engage with culture; and indeed, that you have to engage with culture as part of your task to fill and subdue the earth, and to keep yourself from idols. These things aren't "nice to haves" or "optional extras" in the Christian life—these are biblical commands to obey.

In this final section, I want to show what's possible in terms of Christian cultural analysis. This is the kind of engagement that is needed in order to match the academic analysis that goes on in universities, which is feeding non-Christian worldviews.

No lecturer I know enjoys marking essays, but the cultural analysis assignment I set my students at Oak Hill theological college has verged on the pleasurable. Most of these students have never engaged in theological cultural analysis before, and so the task for them is to culturally analyse one current text or trend using some of the tools I've written about in this book. They can choose anything in the world they want to. Of the hundreds of essays I've assessed over the last decade, topics have ranged from the mundane and predictable to the sublime and ridiculous. As with any student cohort, the quality can be good, bad or ugly. However, I can honestly say that I've learned something new from nearly every paper. It's a thrill to read about something in God's world created by his image-bearers that I've never even heard of, yet which can be connected to and confronted in the gospel of Christ crucified. What's even more exciting is to see disciples of Jesus Christ, my students, starting to interpret the world through sharper and more focused biblical lenses.

The four examples that follow are based on student analyses I've received in recent years. I've edited them down and summarised them using the four stages we've just looked at: Enter, Explore, Expose, and Evangelise.

As you'll quickly realise, reading them is a step up in level from what you've encountered in this book so far—so be warned! However, I want to say two things here:

First, don't freak out! I'm certainly not asking you to write an essay with footnotes that's going to be marked, or something that you are going to formally present to your friends and family—that would be silly. However, I am encouraging you, like my college students, to do some hard work: to start watching and listening closely to what's going on around you, and to look at the world through the word in order to connect and confront your own culture with the gospel of Jesus Christ.

Second, my intention is not that you read these and think, "I could never do that"—in fact, I'm hoping you'll feel the opposite. My aim is to inspire you with what can be achieved given a bit of cultural blood, sweat and tears. You never know, you might read these and think how they could be filled out and improved.

That said, I realise we're all different, with different giftings and strengths—whoever we are, we can all engage with culture in different ways. These examples are at the more academic end of things, but I don't want to make excuses for that. If you're generally interested in social commentary that tries to get to grips with things at depth, then I hope you'll get a lot out of these examples.

That might not be your thing, and that's OK... but then again, it might be. (And how will you know if you don't give them a try?)

So strap yourself in, secure all loose items, and get ready for the thrill-ride that is:

"The ACB of Twitching Zombie Toilets."

# ADULT COLOURING BOOKS

For a struggling publishing industry, it was a welcome relief. In 2015, adult colouring books took the world by storm. Sales numbers skyrocketed all over the planet, and publishers basked in the glow of their quarterly earnings.

The success left many social commentators scratching their heads, however. Who would have thought that so many adults would want to spend their precious spare time colouring? No one had seen this coming. In fact, when Scottish illustrator Johanna Basford pitched her adult colouring book idea to a publisher in 2011, it was met with an awkward silence. Would grown-ups actually buy a book titled *Secret Garden: An Inky Treasure Hunt*? They decided to risk it, however, and published it in 2013. By March 2015 it had sold 10 million copies and had been translated into 40 languages. Before long, countless publishing houses were feverishly printing adult colouring books (ACBs). But why had no one seen this trend coming? What can explain the global popularity of colouring?

## 1. ENTER

Walk into any major bookshop, and you will find a display of ACBs. Their titles usually include phrases like "stress relief" and "colour me calm", so it is little wonder that they are often found alongside books on mindfulness techniques such as yoga, meditation or rhythmic breathing. Like such techniques, ACBs are used by people who want to take a break from their fast-paced digital lives by unplugging and focusing on the present.

Numerous features set ACBs apart from standard mindfulness techniques, however. First of all, they are extremely accessible. There is no need to sign up for a class at the local gym; nor is it necessary to watch YouTube videos to learn any skills. Colouring does not even really require any energy, but can be done at the end of a long day on a sofa or even in bed with a cup of tea. All that is required is a book and a few pens, and if bookstores are out of reach, Amazon is only a click away. Second, whereas standard mindfulness techniques encourage people to become aware of and accept the circumstances they are in, ACBs help people temporarily escape their world and dream of a different one. In order to understand how ACBs do that, it's worth examining the drawings found within their pages.

Interestingly, the drawings rarely depict urban, industrial life. Instead, most feature untainted natural worlds and enchanted lost kingdoms. At the time of writing, the top three most wished for ACBs on Amazon. co.uk, for example, are *Harry Potter*, *Animal Kingdom* and *Enchanted Forest*. Other popular titles include *Lost Ocean*,

*Magical Jungle* and *Romantic Country: Cocot—The Land of Beautiful Towering Castles*. Basford's original book, *Secret Garden: An Inky Treasure Hunt and Coloring Book* (Laurence King, 2013), remains the most popular of all. It is described as "a black and white wonderland", an idyllic world that can "be brought to life through colouring". But why has this proved to be so popular?

When Basford's publishing house took the plunge and published *Secret Garden*, it unwittingly tapped into a massive market: people whose world is "vibrating with anxiety" and who are willing to try all sorts of products and techniques to find peace.[31]

The mindfulness industry already catered to that group, and since colouring was similar to some of its standard techniques, ACBs found themselves a ready audience. However, while colouring's similarities to standard mindfulness techniques paved the way to its acceptance, it was its differences that explain its success. When colouring arrived on the scene, some had already become disillusioned by mainstream meditative practices. As one observer put it, "As much as we are told to go meditate and relax, 9 out of 10 people simply can't do it or [we] try and then wonder if it works."[32]

Meditation also did not always have the desired outcome. Rather than resulting in increased tranquillity, it sometimes led to increased anxiety. As another observer put it, "Focusing on your innermost feelings can be scary. One recent study found that when given the choice, people preferred getting a mild electric shock to being alone with their thoughts."[33] Meditation, it seems, had started to gain the reputation of being hard, and sometimes even counterproductive.

Meditation's weaknesses were colouring's strengths. Using ACBs was easy: the only skill required was one that everyone had acquired in their pre-school days. It also worked for people who felt unable to shut down all their thoughts: it offered "relief and mindfulness without the paralysis that a blank page can cause."[34] Furthermore, it had the reputation of being unusually effective. "Some people [were] adamant that colouring books [were] a path to ... some kind of psychological nirvana."[35] The fact that some of those testimonies actually came from the publishers themselves did not dampen people's enthusiasm. They were eager to try colouring for themselves, and in that way, ACBs became almost an overnight success.

ACBs' popularity "pushed retailers to move quickly to cater to [their] fans."[36] By the end of 2015, 2000 different books were available in the United States alone, and 12 million copies were sold, up from 1 million in the previous year. Before long, people started creating YouTube channels to watch others colour, and used Twitter and Instagram to showcase their drawings. Colouring even "spun off its own bizarre subcultures, like colouring-book parties". In short, "it's hard to overstate the trend."[37]

But what vision do ACBs cast for the world? What do they tell colourers to believe? In order to answer that question, it is worth revisiting the fact that ACBs almost exclusively depict untainted natural worlds. This, in combination with the fact that they are marketed as therapeutic products, indicates that colourers are told that peace is found in a world where people live in close contact with nature. The similarities between the drawings found in ACBs and the designs of 19th-century Art Nouveau artists like William Morris lend support to this argument. Those within this movement were heavily influenced by Romanticism. They felt ill at ease in what they perceived as the ugliness of an increasingly industrialised society, and they longed to live closer to nature, in which could be found freedom, truth and beauty.

It therefore seems plausible that the illustrators of ACBs, like their 19th-century forebears, believe that salvation is found in escape from the ugliness and drudgery of modern life. ACBs encourage colourers to dream of an ideal natural world in order to deal with their anxiety. That world is depicted as one of freedom, rather than of oppression, and it is one in which mankind is surrounded by beauty, rather than ugliness. It is in such a world that colourers are told to seek rest.

## 2. EXPLORE

How do colourers appropriate God's revelation? Positively, it is clear that they believe they were created to dwell in an unspoiled garden-esque kingdom—the kind of paradise we see in Genesis 1 – 2 in the Garden of Eden. Though their words might not express it, their drawings show that they feel this creation has been tainted. This longing for paradise is evidence of being made in the image of God.

Negatively, most ACB users do not acknowledge the existence of a divine being and do not seek salvation in him, but believe they live only in the here and now. According to Charles Taylor, secular people feel "adrift and cast into an anonymous, cold universe." Having closed the door to a bigger reality, they find themselves shut up in a suffocatingly small room, and turn to art to create a space in their minds which allows them to breathe and find peace.[38]

ACBs are therefore used as an escape valve; they are magic wands used to summon up temporary trips to utopia. From this attempt to seek peace in an imaginary natural paradise, it is clear that colourers regard creation as more desirable than the Creator. They do not follow in the footsteps of the psalmist, who longed to "dwell in the house of the LORD all the days of [his] life, to gaze on the beauty of the LORD" (Psalm 27 v 4). Instead, they are convinced that their thirst can be quenched by a world of mystery that exists within their imagination.

What's convenient is that this imaginary paradise is one in which no one has any authority over them. It is a counterfeit of Eden, for it is a garden in which God does not walk. The images, like all idols people create, are mute, and therefore do not impose any moral standards on them. Artists can therefore create their own world, and be their own god. In this way, colouring can even bring about a strange feeling of comfort. As Taylor puts it, "There is a kind of peace in being on [our] own, in solidarity against the blind universe which wrought this horror". It can therefore be concluded that many adults use ACBs to "expand unbelief". Unwilling to acknowledge God's sovereignty, and unable to live as if "a completely flattened universe" is all there is, colouring books are employed to chart a middle way, and thereby sustain unbelief.[39]

## 3. EXPOSE

The problem, of course, is that by colourers' own standards, utopia only exists within the imagination. It is a hope without substance. This has long been recognised by those who come to faith from Eastern backgrounds. The Japanese preacher Taisei Michihata, for example, trained at a Buddhist seminary before his conversion to Christianity. His teachers would often speak of a promised holy land, but "[they] always spoke about things only as they exist in our imagination, as reflections of our longings ... They were merely projections of our own fantasies, the results of religious art."[40]

Therefore, since the desire for a promised land cannot be fulfilled, according to those who only believe in the here and now, it does not actually make sense to use colouring books to reduce anxiety. For what can contemplating an unfulfillable desire ultimately do but lead to despair? If those who use ACBs as an escape valve were consistent, they would seek peace not in colouring but in annihilation. After all, annihilation would result in a permanent escape from this world, rather than only a temporary one. In other words, ACBs suggest that it is possible to have life in an Edenic kingdom without having to surrender your autonomy. In reality, however, that promise comes straight from the lips of the serpent, and leads first to disillusionment, and then to death.

## 4. EVANGELISE

How does Christ subversively fulfil the desires of colourers? Scripture shows that the dream of life in a garden-esque kingdom can become reality. However, it knows nothing of a paradise in which man is autonomous. Instead, it speaks of a paradise that was lost due to the first Adam's desire for sovereignty, and regained by the submission of the "last Adam"—Jesus Christ—to God. Only those who repent from their desire for sovereignty and submit to God will one day dwell in his restored paradise, the new Jerusalem (Revelation 21 v 9-21). Its citizens will live in harmony with nature, rather than being at war with it, and since God will have defeated their enemies, they will be truly free (Isaiah 11 v 6-9).

How then can colouring be redeemed? Those who have repented can use ACBs as visual reminders of the type of land that awaits them, which offers hope to those who feel weighed down by the sorrows of this world. Colouring could also be helpful to Christians who believe that their eternal destiny is a vague, "floaty", disembodied existence in heaven. That misunderstanding of paradise can dull their excitement for eternity. ACBs can therefore be used to help colourers understand the life for which they have been redeemed, so that they press on and persevere in following Jesus. Finally, colouring books can be used to remind believers of the beauty of God himself. For as believers reflect on creation, they cannot help but be reminded of the beauty, the creativity and the power of its Creator. In the end, therefore, colouring can lead believers to worship, for "the heavens declare the glory of God; the skies proclaim the work of his hands" (Psalm 19 v 1).

# BIRDWATCHING

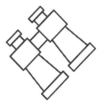

As a family-friendly and wholesome hobby, bird-watching—or "birding" as it is known in some parts of the world—is a popular pastime for an increasing number of people. In this essay we will explore what is going on in people's hearts when they birdwatch.

## 1. ENTER

### What does it say?

Enjoyed by over three million people in the UK, birdwatching is a simple, popular and varied hobby. At its root is "the willingness to look", with the goal of seeing, naming and enjoying the birds.[41] This easy activity takes place in gardens and backyards, in the countryside or at a nature reserve. Indeed, the "British are more obsessed with birds than any other nation on earth",[42] and this is reflected by the growing number who birdwatch, from those who name goldfinches in the garden to those who drive hundreds of miles to glimpse a rare heron. Birdwatching needs no special equipment, although binoculars are helpful. Most birdwatchers will own binoculars or borrow them from a reserve so that the detail of a small bird can be appreciated, making it easier to identify the bird. This enables "intimacy: the delight of being able to observe without being observed".[43] The field guide or "bird book" is a second important tool which equips birdwatchers of all abilities to identify birds. This enhances the enjoyment of seeing something new or different, and provides the language with which to share it with friends.

Conservation is a key part of birdwatching culture, since enjoying nature leads to preserving it. This may be expressed in joining a charity like the American Birding Association or the Royal Society for the Protection of Birds (RSPB); the latter's "large membership of over a million people helps influence national environmental policies".[44] Birdwatchers are also encouraged to help conservation efforts practically. This might be done by feeding birds, participating in survey projects like the annual Big Garden Bird Watch, or signing a petition such as the RSPB's "Letter to the Future".

### Who wrote it?

Many influences and ideas from the last two hundred years have shaped what birdwatching is today. In the UK, perhaps the most significant factor is the rise of the RSPB and its focus on understanding and conserving birds. The RSPB was started in 1889 when a group of affluent women wanted to fight the use of feathers and birds as fashion accessories. By highlighting the suffering of animals, they captured majority opinion, and saw public attitudes shift from exploiting birds to better understanding and therefore protecting them. Today the RSPB has become "one of the world's largest and most influential conservation charities".[45]

Parallel to this, the discipline of ornithology (the study of birds) was transformed by the zoologist Julian Huxley in the early 20th century. He decided to break free from the museum-based study of the past and spent two weeks in 1912 observing birds in the wild; he not only managed to discover many unknown facts about the great crested grebe but also had "the pleasantest of holidays".[46] This inspired others to do likewise and, because of Huxley's background in evolutionary science, linked birdwatching with evolutionary biology. In providing a natural explanation for what looks like patterns in nature designed by God, Darwinian evolution has been the mainstay for biological studies in the last hundred years and is now assumed in museum displays and television documentaries. The result is that humans are no longer seen as set apart from the rest of nature, but rather, are "removed ... from the peak of creation".[47]

A final trend was the increase in suburban gardens in 20th-century Britain. The creation of four million homes with gardens between 1920 and 1939 created a network of semi-woodland habitat, which supports many species of birds, in the very places where we live. This emphasis on gardens was the continuation of a passionate Victorian idea that we must live close to nature in order to have a good quality of life.

## Who reads it?

Given this backdrop, what are birdwatchers being encouraged to do, think and believe, and how do they respond to that?

Celebrity birdwatchers tell birdwatchers that they themselves are part of nature. Human beings are just "one more species". In fact, "we are hairless apes". We share the environment with birds, and our story is the same evolutionary story as that of the birds around us. Each form of life is considered "equally valid, equally important". As a part of nature, our first need is to enjoy our world. Birds are seen as a great source of this enjoyment since they are part of nature and yet "creatures apart", and appear almost magical because they can fly. Birds have always occupied a special role of bringing wonder in an entirely natural world: "Ever since humans first walked upright, they were able ... to observe the birds."[48]

Identifying the names of birds enhances this enjoyment and helps to capture our imagination. A name also "demonstrates the existence of a shared concept". As we name the bird, not only can we share the experience of seeing it with others but we also feel that the bird has shared something with us—essentially we inhabit the same world. Hence a birdwatcher who catches a glimpse of an exciting bird he knows can say, "I see the flash, I don't have to wonder what it is. And mine is the heart that leaps".[49]

The second need underlying birdwatching is the need to reconnect with nature by looking after it. We are told that we have become the one species that is set apart for the wrong reason—we harm nature. Conservation and bird-feeding are therefore important as they appear to redeem us in some way, by bringing us closer to nature, benefitting rather than destroying it. This portrayal of conservation as a deep need is seen when it is talked of as "a religion, a moral crusade and a political commitment".[50]

Within the birdwatching culture there are signs of both compliance with and rebellion against these messages from the birdwatching media. The creation of an entire bird-food industry now worth £200 million a year, the increase of RSPB membership to over a million people, and the rise in the number of TV programmes about birdwatching all show there is significant demand for enjoying and understanding birds.

However, birdwatchers have habits which don't always sit well with the birdwatching elite. Some celebrity birdwatchers bemoan the fact that many people stay in the garden to watch birds rather than getting out; or regret the way in which others turn birdwatching into a competition, "twitching", to see the highest number of birds.[51]

Most interestingly, rebellion against the given narrative is seen in the tendency to assign human characteristics to birds; for many birdwatchers there are good birds, such as blue tits, and bad birds, such as magpies. This feeds back to elicit a strong reteaching of the "correct" narrative in the birdwatching media. Simon Barnes, for example, says that magpies "are not trying to be humans", and that people need to realise that nature is not there for our delight, and we are a part of nature, not its master.[52] The birdwatcher is taught to see him- or herself as part of a world that is not meaningful or beautiful, but just is.

## 2. EXPLORE

Though birdwatching is a product of a culture that largely doesn't know God, through his common grace there is still in it a revelation of God's love towards his creation. One example of this is the joy that people experience in seeing the beauty of the created world. It is true that the heart does indeed leap at the glory in creation, because God has given to all his creatures a world whose beauty "far outdistances any work of art that humans can produce".[53]

This common grace is also reflected in the enjoyment of identifying birds. As Turnau notes, "As God created the world, when we do culture, we create shared worlds of meaning that we mutually inhabit".[54] Hence the shared meaning enjoyed when identifying and talking about birds is testimony to God's grace in giving us the capacity to be creative. Our God-given role in creation is also shown by the emphasis on conservation. This accords with the Bible's insistence that man was placed in God's world to "work it and take care of it" (Genesis 2 v 15). Such stewardship is part of what it is to be human, and it is satisfying to exercise that role and look after the created order.

However, the narrative that underpins birdwatching is also idolatrous. The response to God's provision of a beautiful world is to cut out God, the main protagonist in the story, and to "refuse to recognize this home of ours as a gift".[55] Even if God is referred to, it is not as the sovereign Creator, but rather, as an alternative name for natural processes.[56] The problems in the natural world are written up as the way nature is or a reflection of humanity spoiling the creation, and are not heeded as a warning from God as his revelation should be.

Sinful humanity repeatedly writes over God's good messages too. Removing God from the story is attractive as it removes the "need for repentance to a personal God".[57] We see this in the way the birdwatching media want to make humans the same as the other creatures, rather than embracing God's message that we are in a position of wonderful responsibility over his creation (Psalm 8 v 6). This leads people to seek "the source and provision of what we need either physically or emotionally in ... something other than the one true God",[58] which is idolatry.

In birdwatching this means finding meaning in evolution, which itself always has religious connotations. Indeed idols are counterfeits of God, faking his identity and character. Evolution is a counterfeit religion which has a provision in the past (the evolution of life) and the prospect of blessing or curse in the future (the plight of nature), both of which shape me morally in the present. All of this counterfeits what it looks like to be in a relationship with the true God.

### 3 & 4. EXPOSE AND EVANGELISE

The idolatrous nature of the text is shown by the ways in which it cannot help us meet our real needs. The delight at a beautiful bird, that moment "when entertainment and wonder happen",[59] can be worship, which is seeking uncreated glory in a created thing. Hence it doesn't satisfy, leading people to want to see the next impressive bird or to become competitive. This problem should make us realise that "God's work in creation ... testifies that he is the fountain of all happiness", and move us to find our joy in beholding and knowing him.[60] Conservation also betrays this failure, as it is often done in an attitude of desperation or hostility, as shown by Barnes' comment that "we live in a world working up to an ecological holocaust".[61] In a world where watching the birds should teach us that God provides for all his creatures (Matthew 6 v 26), stewardship can be done in dependence on a God, who is sovereign and good.

The birdwatching narrative also contains dissatisfying contradictions. One writer says that "nature is not beautiful; nature only is", yet asks in the same book, "Why are we so keen on its beauties?"[62] If there is no God, the only reason we hold on to beauty and joy is "that we want to believe that [nature] is more than ... evolutionary survival strategy". The contradiction shows that "we know that it is more, something pointing to a deeper spiritual reality."[63]

The birdwatching narrative seeks to enjoy the rich blessings of God's world while cutting out the Provider. However, when we look at nature through the glasses of Scripture, we find a story that makes sense of the fallenness of the world and our desire to create meaning and look after it. And we also find the God who made it and placed us over it, and who is the "spiritual beauty that it represents", in whom we will find full satisfaction.

# ZOMBIES: "THEY'RE US!"

On 23rd October 2011, the news reported that 3000 zombies had overrun the streets of Brighton, UK. This wasn't strictly fake news. The invasion was real; the zombies, however, were not. They were, in fact, 3000 zombiephiles participating in the latest craze, the ZomMob: people of all ages and backgrounds, dressed as zombies, assembling to "shuffle" through major cities. One article observes, "It's the latest proof ... that the undead are really on the march—culturally at least". Over the last five decades, there has been a huge growth in literature mentioning zombies. What is the appeal behind this cultural phenomenon?

In this essay we will restrict our analysis to the filmmaker George A. Romero's zombie—the "RomZom"— as portrayed in films including *Night of the Living Dead* (1968), *Dawn of the Dead* (1978) and *Day of the Dead* (1985). Romero is considered to be the father of the modern zombie film; Twohy asserts that he "made sure that zombies would never be seen the same way again".[64]

## 1. ENTER
### What does it say?

Although the idea of the dead eating the living was not entirely new,[65] *Night of the Living Dead* (1968) was the first film to imagine this in the form of the zombie. "*Night* ... introduced cannibalistic features into 'living dead' representation,"[66] "creating a new breed of zombie significantly more terrifying than previous depictions."[67]

RomZom is "a slow, reanimated, flesh-hungry corpse usually occurring within a mob";[68] a "ghoulish plague monster",[69] robbed of intellect and emotion.[70] It is depicted as "threaten[ing and infecting] the entire human race",[71] zombifying victims, usually within an apocalyptic context. In fact, "more than any other monster, zombies ... signal the end of the world as we have known it".[72]

Furthermore, according to Paffenroth, RomZom was designed to straddle "the boundary between ... human and sub-human."[73] Citing *Night* as an example, Wilson puts it this way: "The rare horror film ... blurs the boundaries ... between darkness and light", so that the "protagonist find[s] the real monster" inside them.[74] Here, we find Romero's intention: he is "asking what is a smart zombie, other than ... a human being [enslaved] to its appetites? Or what are we, other than ... slightly smart zombies, a tribe of deranged, self-destructive cannibals preying on one another?"[75]

### Who wrote it?

Romero is a fun-loving man. During a self-satirising advertisement for one of his films, he says he "hopes [we] have fun watching it".[76] But he is also a suspicious man, believing that our neighbours are our worst enemies and that the three television networks of his day were the "three big lies ... now there are 400,000 bloggers ... there are 400,000 potential lies".[77] He admits that he has used his films to "express [his] political views". He pessimistically confesses that "the humans [in his films] are the [characters] I dislike the most ... they're where the trouble really lies. The zombies are just mosquitoes".[78] Plot devices, such as reserving the worst behaviour for human characters, portray Romero's mistrust of humanity, and again raise the question of "What are we?"[79]

Romero, therefore, intends the zombie to expose the state of humanity, especially ills like consumerism, individualism and rationalism. Paffenroth remarks that "anyone who watches zombie movies must be prepared for a strong indictment of life in modern America".[80] The zombie, then, is a multi-level metaphor or mirror for true humanity.

### Who reads it?

In spite of the initial outcry against *Night* (1968), the film has proved to be exceedingly popular across cultures and generations. The following extract from *Varsity* encapsulates the early response.

> Until the Supreme Court establishes clear-cut
> guidelines for the pornography of violence, Night
> ... will serve nicely as an outer-limit definition
> by example ... This horror film ... casts serious
> aspersions on the integrity and social responsibility

of its ... makers ... and about the moral health of filmgoers who cheerfully opt for this unrelieved orgy of sadism.[81]

However, "reviewers began to recognise that the film did not just shock and disgust ... it disturbed and perplexed viewers, and demanded more of them at some deeper, more thoughtful ... level".[82] By the time *Dawn of the Dead* was released (1978), critics were subjecting Romero's films to "detailed and scholarly analysis".[83] Romero's messages seemed to be getting through to viewers too. Harper describes how, on visiting a mall after viewing *Dawn*, one fan exclaimed, "Look! It's just like *Dawn*! All of these shoppers look like zombies walking about the place!"[84] The growth in zombie films in the last four decades demonstrates the broad appeal of RomZom.[85]

Due to RomZom's resemblance to humans, it has become the subject of research and debate among philosophers. It has fascinated various academics, such as Dr Leaning of Winchester University, UK, who now offers a module on the zombie.[86] Film commentators speculate about multiple metaphors behind RomZom. In this essay we will consider four such metaphors offered by Michael Johnson, from *ReelSchool*: disassociation, true humanity, death and contagion.[87]

The themes of disassociation, contagion and death relate. Johnson explains that the zombie resonates with our desires to remain individual when facing social pressure to conform, and to "disassociate" or set ourselves apart from the crowd; the relentless hordes of zombies are a picture of those forces that seek to contaminate us with ideas. Dennett agrees that zombies represent the proponents of any worldview. For example, Christians could be thought of as zombies, presenting a threat; the gospel, then, becomes a contagion.[88] This tends to be linked to the fear of death and viral contamination: the zombie is "a literal representation of our future, forcing you to face your fear ... literally coming slowly toward you, unrelenting, uncompromising, unstoppable". Again, Romero's message comes to the fore; Johnson says "one of the most terrifying aspects [of the zombie genre] ... has nothing to do with the monster outside trying to beat down your door; it has everything to do with the monster within. In a post-apocalyptic world ... people are free to be *who they really are*".[89]

As Johnson suggests, the appeal of zombies also reflects a human fantasy of living through an apocalypse. Cole, for example, suggests that the zombie film "indulg[es] our post-apocalyptic fantasies".[90] The ZomMob mentioned in the introduction affords the opportunity to live the apocalypse fantasy somewhat, as groups re-enact attacks and conversions. Video games protagonise us in our own zombie apocalypse.[91] Event organisers Battlefield Live offer more realistic apocalyptic experiences "by popular demand".[92] One article on cracked.com suggests that the reason why this fantasy "appeals to us [is] because there's nobody left to judge us ... the apocalypse is like being released from a prison".[93] Another offers five reasons; arguably, they all spring from the desire for autonomy.[94]

## 2. EXPLORE

Having described the cultural text and its world, we are now able to subject it to our theological analysis.

Jonathan Edwards says that from general revelation (looking at the world around us) we can conclude that "... all mankind are by nature in a state of total ruin".[95] Romero has come to the same conclusion. In some ways, Romero's films amplify God's revelation about the true state of humanity. In this respect, the zombie is the product of common grace and general revelation. The apostle Paul uses imagery that we might call "zombiesque" to describe the behaviour of fallen humanity who "bite and devour one another" (Galatians 5 v 15). Similarly, Romero sees humanity "bite and devour one another", portrays this in the form of zombies, and says, in effect, *They're us*. By establishing a cause for the zombies' evil, and contrasting the zombies with the human characters, he asks the viewer, "What disease causes your evil?" His films recognise and proclaim that we shouldn't be this way, which is in line with God's intention. Romero's portrayal of man's tendency to evil is a sign of God's restraining grace and general revelation.

Embodying and magnifying humanity's evils in this way has meant that zombies, in context, function similarly to God's law. Paul writes that he "would not have known what sin was had it not been for the law" (Romans 7 v 7). Luther likens the law to a mirror "in which you will find what you lack and what you should seek".[96] The zombie is like the law, not the gospel—a mirror exposing the need for a saviour, yet offering no saviour. In contrast, Edwards writes that "Christ stands in direct relation to this ruin, as the remedy to the disease".[97] The zombie does not go this far, nor does it offer an alternative; therefore it offers no hope.

Brockway suggests that autonomy is at the root of the apocalyptic fantasy. This desire for control is at the heart of idolatry, and originates in the Garden of Eden in Adam and Eve's decision to eat the fruit. This means that our fascination with the zombie apocalypse both stems from and provokes our longings to live out our deep idol of autonomy.

There may be something else at work here too, however. Davidson suggests that the zombie fantasy massages another yearning: to be set free from the prison of the busyness of life and work. This echoes Lamech's cry that his son, Noah, "will comfort us in the labour and painful toil of our hands" (Genesis 5 v 29). Lamech longs for the end of painful work—a longing for the deliverance from the curse. Perhaps we find ourselves captivated by the zombie apocalypse because it scratches this itch, arousing hope of an end. The human spirit longs for a saviour to give us deliverance from the curse, giving us rest. However, ultimately this fantasy becomes idolatry, as it sets up an apocalypse as salvation.

### 3 & 4. EXPOSE AND EVANGELISE

We have found that RomZom has layers of meaning which go further and deeper than Romero intended. It reveals our depravity; it massages our inner longings or idolatries, and provides a means of externalising them or simply our misgivings. This is significant, because viewers who are persuaded by RomZom would not need to be persuaded  to acknowledge humanity's sinful inclination and aberration; in this respect, their hearts might prove to be good soil for the seed of the gospel. Furthermore, RomZom shows that they are longing—longing for life, rest and deliverance from the curse—and feeling hopeless and imprisoned. Through the zombie we arrive at the need for a saviour, and so, through the zombie, we arrive at Christ: "God, who is rich in mercy, made us alive with Christ even when we were dead in transgressions" (Ephesians 2 v 4-5).

# THE JAPANESE DOMESTIC TOILET*

Travellers to Japan often express horror at traditional Asian squat-toilets, sometimes characterised—especially in parks and train stations—by "the four Ks... *kiken* (dangerous), *kitanai* (dirty), *kurai* (dark) and *kasai* [sic] (stinky)".[98] However, they are usually impressed by the advanced bidet-toilets known as Washlets found both in many homes and in public conveniences in hotels and department stores.[99]

## 1. ENTER
### What does it say?
Chun describes these toilets as follows: "There are buttons to open the lid and/or seat, buttons to spray front or bottom, controls to set water temperature and

---

* This might seem a rather obscure choice. I've included it as an example of crosscultural analysis, which is crucial in our diverse and connected world. As you will see, what we in the West might just think is a functional process and a world away from "religion", is to other cultures profoundly "religious" in nature. Think about similar examples that might be applicable to your Muslim, Hindu or Sikh neighbours.

back and forth pulsation. Most have automatic blow-dryers and warm seats (for winter use), and some have electronically triggered catalytic deodorisers and stain-resistant porcelain coatings that permit the toilet to clean itself."[100] Women's public toilets are also often equipped with a "Sound Princess" gadget, which makes flushing sounds or plays music to mask the embarrassing sounds of urination.[101]

Whenever space considerations allow, a domestic toilet is situated in a separate room from the bathroom. A special pair of slippers is provided for the toilet room for one to change into on entering. While some people, for reasons of health and hygiene, retain the squat style of toilet in their homes, most now have a Western-style "sit-toilet". Half of Japanese houses have some kind of Washlet, as described above.[102] If there is no electric seat-warmer, the seat will probably have a cover for warmth. This, and the mat, handtowel, lid-cover and toilet-roll cover usually present are in a colour or design that reflects the season. Decoration is provided by some pictures or a calendar, and possibly flowers or pebbles. A bookshelf is very rare. Air-freshener is likely to be a tree- or woodland-type fragrance.[103]

## Who wrote it?

As we consider the Japanese domestic toilet, we will look at its situation in the house, Shinto concepts of purity and safety, ideas of beauty and health, and the use of technology.

The position of a toilet is governed by elaborate rules drawn largely from Chinese *fengshui*, which is based on

Taoist philosophy. The word *fengshui* is written with the characters for "wind" and "water", and its aim is to manipulate the flow of life energy caused by the interplay of the five elements (water, metal, fire, earth and wood) with yin (matter) and yang (spirit).[104] Following these rules is supposed to result in health and prosperity for all members of the household. In fact, the rules are so complicated, Kalland explains, that 80 percent compliance when building a house is considered high, and therefore additional rituals are further required to prevent calamity.[105]

The locations of running water and of "dirty" toilets, kitchens and hearths are particularly important. For example, it's thought that toilets placed in the northeast, southwest or northwest sections will adversely affect household members associated with those sections.[106] *Fengshui* suggests that a toilet lid should be kept shut to prevent the escape of life force, so the sensors on a Washlet, which open the lid as someone approaches and close it when they leave, represent a new solution to an old problem. Flowers or pebbles in the toilet room are an "earth" element which counteracts the water's "flushing away" of life force and hence prosperity.

These originally Taoist rules, originating in China, have been incorporated into folk Shinto, the indigenous Japanese religious tradition. So next we turn to consider an important way in which the toilet is influenced by Shinto.

A major concern of Shinto is with purity. Impurity arises from many actions and circumstances, and, unlike sin, is not always connected to human moral responsibility. As in many societies, cleanliness and purity are associated with safety, and impurity or pollution with danger. For example, the actions of rinsing the mouth and washing the hands are typically performed on entering shrine precincts and on returning home from outside. This distinction between "inside"—which is "clean" and "safe"—and "outside"—"dirty" and "dangerous"—is an important one for the Japanese, and learnt from a very early age. It illustrates Mary Douglas' famous assertion that uncleanness is "matter out of place" and therefore to be approached through order.[107] The toilet is a "dirty" place, and order is imposed by setting a boundary between it and the rest of the house, symbolised by changing into slippers. This also explains the preference for having a separate toilet and bathroom.

The toilet's "dirtiness" accounts for the danger associated with it, and the care taken over its positioning. McElligott also tells the story of a neighbour desperate to find the site of the toilet among the ashes of a totally burned-down house in his street, because he felt the "spirit of the toilet" had to be appeased to avert calamity.[108] Horan suggests the preference for a tree-scented air-freshener in the bathroom relates to the fact that nanten trees used to be planted near to privies to attract a fictitious creature which would make bad dreams disappear.[109] On launching the Washlet in the early 1980s, the manufacturer TOTO appealed in their advertising to the Japanese obsession with cleanliness, which partly arises from this Shinto tradition. Chun quotes a TOTO promotional video: "The Japanese are a nation of people who like to wash their bottoms".[110]

Other elements of the Japanese toilet room are interesting to note. For example, while we have seen that some of the beautification of the toilet room is connected to *fengshui* beliefs, elements such as the seasonal decorations reflect the fact that nature is considered beautiful in Japan. This concern with the pursuit of beauty in wider Japanese culture has been noted by many observers.[111] The Washlet is also considered to promote health. The anal washing and drying is supposedly useful in easing constipation and haemorrhoids, and recent models can measure urine sugar, body weight and even body fat.

Finally, the toilet demonstrates the Japanese use and improvement of technologies to deal with problems produced by cultural concerns, such as health and "safety". By distancing the user from bodily functions, it can also be considered a means of covering embarrassment and ensuring dignity. The Washlet is actually a much-improved version of an original 1960s American model designed for use in hospitals, and so is an example of Japan leading the way on production of objects that are both practical and beautiful.[112] Lundell links this pursuit of excellence with the senses of national superiority and perfectionism.[113]

## Who reads it?

The vision of what it is to be a good human being is implicit in much of what we have seen above. Such a person is concerned with purity and order, of which bodily cleanliness is only one part. A pure heart in

Japan is not directed by moral absolutes, but expressed, McElligott suggests, in "sincerity", which involves doing things in "the right way" as determined by established and accepted practice.[114] Sincerity is also shown by making efforts to behave with courtesy and empathy. Such behaviour preserves harmony in relationships with the human and non-human world.

Offering a clean and safe place for the satisfaction of the basic needs to urinate and defecate, as well as preserving dignity, is therefore a courteous act towards others. Making efforts to site the toilet properly reflects a concern to bring health and prosperity to the household, but also, more widely, to live in harmony with the cosmos, and to keep ancestral and community spirits content. The good life is also one of beauty, including sensitivity to seasons and to nature. It guards health as a way of avoiding causing worry or trouble to others. It uses technology in serving humans and the environment.

## 2. EXPLORE

The worldview seen here believes in the basic goodness of humankind, and the goodness and abundance of nature. It also assumes a continuity between the human and non-human elements of reality, including the dead—who are in some sense "still with us"—along with myriad other spirits indwelling and protecting Japan.

While the Japanese share to some extent in the modern narrative of progress both scientific and social (hence the enthusiastic adoption of technologies), there is a deeper sense of time which is not linear. Time is both a constantly evaporating present moment and a cycle. The past too is always present, but also forgotten.[115] Taoist influence means that, for the Japanese, time is not equal—there are auspicious and inauspicious days and years. In Taoist philosophy the fundamental desires are for harmony and purity. Humankind has some role in maintaining harmony, but fate, or "the way things turn out", plays a large part. In this worldview, humans exist as part of a harmonious cosmos, but the biblical idea of their being in any sense special—separate from and with authority over other elements—is rejected.

In the Japanese toilet we see concerns for family, community and the environment which reflect something of God's good creation of humanity in the image of God. The first people were created to be in relationship with others, and to work and keep the place they lived in (Genesis 1 v 27; 2 v 15, 18). The desire to make even the toilet beautiful further adds to this.

On the other hand, the revelation of common grace is suppressed when health, prosperity and safety, given as signs of God's blessing to be responded to in thanks, are not received as such. Instead, they are seen as something to be achieved by human techniques and manipulation. The categories of impurity and danger, and of embarrassment at bodily functions, reflect something of a sense of things gone wrong, but any awareness of the wrath of a holy Creator God is also suppressed. Again, human technologies, whether ancient *fengshui* or modern gadgets, are used to deal with the "dangerous".

In Japanese domestic toilets we find a focus on technology, health, cleanliness and safety—these were intended as God-given means by which to control and subdue the earth, making it a better place in which to live, in health and prosperity. However, the obsessions surrounding cleanliness and technology with regards to the Japanese toilet show that these have become idols.[116]

### 3 & 4. EXPOSE AND EVANGELISE

Against Taoism, we must affirm that all time and space is equal, because all are equally under the lordship of Christ (Matthew 28 v 18). Against the story of Japanese uniqueness, of which we have seen hints here, we need to affirm that God has created all nations, and promises that representatives from every nation will be present in the new creation (Acts 17 v 26; Revelation 7 v 9). The needs expressed in the Japanese worldview as outlined and analysed above are both subverted and fulfilled in the gospel of Jesus Christ.

The obsessiveness of the pursuit of technology, cleanliness and safety is itself a demonstration that these idols cannot satisfy, and cannot be a substitute for God. The gospel offers a clean heart—pure at the deepest, most inward, level, such that there is no shame in standing even before a holy God (Hebrews 10 v 19-22). Whereas *fengshui* is believed to offer, at best, 80% protection from household calamities, the human need for safety is fully met in God, who is a refuge for his people (Psalm 46 v 1). The never-satisfied longings for health and prosperity in this world can be shown to be weak and feeble in comparison to the eternal life and imperishable, unfading inheritance promised in the new creation (1 Peter 1 v 3-4). Scripture promises that this will be a place of beauty, abundance and harmony far exceeding Japanese longings for these things. Christians alone can speak rightly of harmony, peace and reconciliation, because Christians alone know the God who brings harmony, first in our relationship with him, then in our relationships with one another, and finally with all creation (Romans 5 v 1; Isaiah 11 v 6-9).

# ENDNOTES

## Intro

1   https://www.theguardian.com/music/2015/jun/10/miley-cyrus-i-dont-relate-to-being-boy-or-girl.

2   Anthony Thwaite, https://www.spectator.co.uk/2015/06/oh-dear/. Used with permission.

## Chapter 1

3   Edward Jewitt Robinson, *The Daughters of India: Their Social Condition, Religion, Literature, Obligations, and Prospects* (T. Murray, 1860), p 131.

4   J.H. Bavinck, quoted in Paul Visser, *Heart for the Gospel, Heart for the World: The Life and Thought of Reformed Pioneer Missiologist Johan Herman Bavinck (1895-1964)* (Wipf&Stock, 2003), p 286.

5   James Sire, *Naming the Elephant* (InterVarsity Press, 2015), p 112.

6   The philosopher in question is Charles Taylor, who, more than anyone, has described this way of thinking about the secular. He's not an easy read. If you are interested, you might look at James K.A. Smith, *How (Not) to Be Secular: Reading Charles Taylor* (Eerdmans, 2014).

7   *Abraham Kuyper: A Centennial Reader*, ed. James D. Bratt (Eerdmans, 1998), p 488.

## Chapter 2

8   John M. Frame, *The Doctrine of the Christian Life* (Presbyterian

and Reformed, 2008), p 857.

9     Henry Van Til, *The Calvinistic Concept of Culture* (Baker, 2001), p 200.

10     Bavinck, "Religious Consciousness", *The J.H. Bavinck Reader*, ed. John Bolt, James D. Bratt and P. J. Visser, trans. James A. De Jong (William B. Eerdmans Publishing Company, 2013), p 279.

11     Greg Beale, *We Become What We Worship* (IVP, 2008), p 16.

12     Jonathan Leeman, *Political Church: The Local Assembly As Embassy of Christ's Rule* (Apollos, 2016), p 14, 92.

13     Bavinck, quoted in Brian G. Mattson, *Restored to Our Destiny: Eschatology and the Image of God in Herman Bavinck's Reformed Dogmatics* (Brill, 2011), p 5.

14     Brian Mattson, *Cultural Amnesia* (Swinging Bridge Press, 2018), p 33-34.

## Chapter 3

15     J.H. Bavinck, *The Church Between Temple and Mosque* (Eerdmans, 1966), p 33.

16     Grant Horner, *Meaning at the Movies* (Crossway, 2010), p 47.

## Chapter 4

17     A really great book which shows these patterns is by Christopher Watkin, *Thinking Through Creation* (P&R, 2017).

18     C.S. Lewis, *The Weight of Glory* (HarperCollins, 2009), p 91-92.

19     Mike Cosper, *The Stories We Tell* (Crossway, 2014), from p 52.

20     John Calvin, *Institutes*, 3.11.1.

21     Glynn Harrison makes this point in *A Better Story* (IVP, 2016).

22     Cal Newport makes this point in *Deep Work: Rules for Focused Success in a Distracted World* (Paitkus, 2016).

23     John Piper, "Twelve questions to ask before you watch *Game of Thrones*", https://www.desiringgod.org/articles/12-questions-to-ask-before-you-watch-game-of-thrones.

24     See Andrew David Naselli and J.D. Crowley, *Conscience: What It Is, How to Train It, and Loving Those Who Differ* (Crossway, 2016).

## Chapter 7

25     One excellent little book on the art of asking penetrating questions is Greg Koukl, *Tactics* (Zondervan, 2009).

26     Taken from Daniel Strange, "Reflections on Gospel Contextual-

ization" in Timothy Keller, *Loving the City* (Zondervan, 2016), from p 94.

27  Ted Turnau, "Popular Culture, Apologetics and the Discourse of Desire", *Cultural Encounters* 8:2 (Nov. 2012), p 25-46.

28  Gary Parkinson, "It's Coming Home: Why Three Lions is such an important song in English football culture", https://www. fourfourtwo.com/features/its-coming-home-why-three-lions-such-important-song-english-football-culture.

29  https://www.thesun.co.uk/world-cup-2018/6694139/how-many-watch-world-cup-2018-viewing-figures-england-croatia/.

30  https://heirsmagazine.com/articles/the-world-cup-england-and-you.

## Adult colouring books

31  Zoe Williams, "Adult Colouring-in Books: The Latest Weapon against Stress and Anxiety", https://www.theguardian.com/books/2015/jun/26/adult-colouring-in-books-anxiety-stress-mindfulness.

32  Eloise Keating, "Businesses Turn to Colouring Books for Employees: Are They the Key to a Stress-Free Workplace?" n.p. Online: http://www.smartcompany.com.au/people-humanresources/leadership/46363-businesses-turn-to-colouring-books-for-employees-are-they-the-key-to-a-stress-free-workplace/.

33  Matthew Hutson, "People Prefer Electric Shocks to Being Alone With Their Thoughts", http://www.theatlantic.com/health/archive/2014/07/people-prefer-electric-shocks-to-being-alone-with-their-thoughts/373936/.

34  Julie Beck, "The Zen of Adult Coloring Books", http://www.theatlantic.com/health/archive/2015/11/sorry-benedict-cumberbatch-your-head-is-fine/414010/.

35  Heather Schwedel, "Coloring Books for Adults: We Asked Therapists for Their Opinions", https://www.theguardian.com/lifeandstyle/2015/aug/17/coloring-books-adults-therapists-opinions.

36  Sarah Halzack, "The Big Business behind the Adult Coloring Book Craze", https://www.washingtonpost.com/business/economy/the-big-business-behind-the-adult-coloringbook-craze/2016/03/09/ccf241bc-da62-11e5-891a-4ed04f4213e8_story.html.

37  Thu-Huong Ha, "America's Obsession with Adult Coloring Is a Cry for Help", http://qz.com/650378/the-sad-reason-american-adults-are-so-obsessed-with-coloring-books/

38  Charles Taylor, *A Secular Age* (Harvard University Press, 2007), p

64, 71, 307, 309.

39   Taylor, *A Secular Age*, p 306.

40   J.H. Bavinck, *The J.H. Bavinck Reader*, p 135-36.


## Birdwatching

41   Simon Barnes, *How to Be a Bad Birdwatcher: To the Greater Glory of Life* (Short Books, 2004), p 16. It is interesting to note that birdwatching is a much more widely enjoyed hobby than the common perception allows. In fact the competitive side, often called "twitching", is not to be thought of as the realm of the "best" but simply competitive people involved in a hobby that usually focuses on enjoyment (p 21).

42   TV: Stephen Moss and Susie Painter, *Birds Britannia 1: Garden Birds* (BBC 4 7/11/10), 0.04.

43   Barnes, p 48.

44   Peter Holden and Tim Cleeves, *RSPB Handbook of British Birds* (A&C Black, 2008), p 6.

45   Holden and Cleeves, p 6.

46   Julian Huxley, "The Courtship Habits of the Great Crested Grebe", *Proceedings of the Zoological Society of London* 84 (1914), p. 492.

47   Kirsten Birkett, *The Essence of Darwinism* (Matthias Media, 2001), p 119.

48   Barnes, p 154, 63, 30, 29.

49   Barnes, p 83, 85.

50   Barnes, p 191.

51   So Bill Oddie despairs, "For an awful lot of people there [are] nothing but garden birds"; see TV: Stephen Moss and Susie Painter, *Birds Britannia 1*, 1.34. And Simon Barnes writes that twitchers "are not the orthodoxy ... they are not what birdwatchers want to be in their heart of hearts," See Barnes, p 21.

52   Barnes, p 153-154.

53   Stephen J. Nichols, *Jonathan Edwards: A Guided Tour of His Life and Thought* (P&R, 2001), p 169.

54   Theodore A. Turnau III, "Equipping Students to Engage Popular Culture", p 135-157 in *The Word of God for the Academy in Contemporary Culture(s)* [Reprinted with page numbers 1 - 28], edited by John B. Hulst and Peter Balla (Karoli Gaspar Reformed University Press, 2003), p 4.

55   Turnau, "Reflecting Theologically on Popular Culture as Meaningful," p 289.

56 So Barnes: "God, or evolution, or whatever you want to call the process has come up with these two different species." Barnes, *How to Be a Bad Birdwatcher*, p 39.
57 Turnau, "Reflecting Theologically on Popular Culture as Meaningful", *Calvin Theological Journal* 37 (2002), p 290.
58 Scott J. Hafemann, *The God of Promise and the Life of Faith: Understanding the Heart of the Bible* (Crossway, 2001), p 35.
59 Turnau, "Equipping Students to Engage Popular Culture", p 8.
60 Nichols, p 170.
61 Barnes, p 151.
62 Barnes, p 154, 159.
63 Turnau, "Equipping Students to Engage Popular Culture", p 23.

## Zombies: "They're Us!"

64 Margaret Twohy, "From Voodoo to Viruses: The Evolution of the Zombie in Twentieth Century Popular Culture", Master's thesis (Trinity College Dublin, 2008), p 13.
65 The dead returning to eat the living has long been in man's consciousness. The Epic of Gilgamesh contains these words: "I shall raise up the dead, and they will eat the living. I shall make the dead outnumber the living!" Quotes by Stephanie Dalley, *Myths from Mesopotamia: Creation, the Flood, Gilgamesh, and Others* (Revised, Oxford University Press, 2009), p 80.
66 Tony Williams, *The Cinema of George A. Romero: Knight of the Living Dead* (Wallflower Press, 2003), p 12.
67 Twohy, p 15.
68 Twohy, p 15.
69 James B. Twitchell, *Dreadful Pleasures: An Anatomy of Modern Horror* (Oxford University Press, 1985), p 267.
70 Kim Paffenroth, *Gospel of the Living Dead: George Romero's Visions of Hell on Earth* (Baylor University Press, 2006), p 12.
71 "Zombie (fictional) - Wikipedia, the free encyclopaedia," https://en.wikipedia.org/wiki/Zombie.
72 Paffenroth, p 8.
74 Eric G. Wilson, *Secret Cinema: Gnostic Vision in Film (Bloomsbury Academic, 2006)*, from p 121.
75 Paffenroth, p 7.
76 "*Survival of the Dead* George A. Romero Introduction", 2010, [cited 13 November 2011]. Online: http://www.youtube.com/watch?v=9sGx0gTVkqM&feature=youtube_gdata_player.
77 "*Diary of the Dead*—George A. Romero interview", 2007, [cited

13 November 2011]. Online: http://www.youtube.com/watch?v=lj OVL8lCV_Q&feature=youtube_gdata_player.

78  "10 Questions for George Romero", [cited 13 November 2011]. Online: http://www.time.com/time/magazine/article/0,9171,1992390,00.html.

79  Paffenroth, p 12.

80  Paffenroth, p 21.

81  Paffenroth, p 27. Ironically, but for different reasons, was this not Romero's intent—to cast aspersions on the moral health of the filmgoers?

82  Paffenroth, p 28.

83  Paffenroth, p 28.

84  Harper, "Zombies, Malls, and the Consumerism Debate: George Romero's Dawn of the Dead," *Americana: The Journal of American Popular Culture (1990-present)* 1 (2002), http://www. americanpopularculture.com/journal/articles/fall_2002/harper. htm.

85  "The Internet Movie Database (IMDb)," n.p. [cited 13 November 2011]. Online: http://www.imdb.com/. Besides the many American titles, Canada has produced *Shivers* (1975) and *Rabid* (1977); New Zealand/UK produced *Braindead* (1992); there is Italy's *Dellamorte Dellamore* (1994); Japan's *Versus* (2000); England's *28 Days Later* (2002) and *Shaun of the Dead* (2004); and Spain's *[Rec]* (2007). Some titles have been distributed under different names in the Philippines and Portugal.

86  John Sudworth, "Zombie Craze Continues to Infect Popular Culture" [cited 13 November 2011]. Online: https://www.bbc.co.uk/ news/uk-15418899.

87  Michael Johnson, "The Meaning of the Zombie", YouTube [cited 13 November 2011]. Online: http://www.youtube.com/watch?v=_ nyEQplt9Nc.

88  "Dan Dennett on Dangerous Memes", video on TED.com [cited 13 November 2011]. Online: http://www.ted.com/talks/lang/eng/ dan_dennett_on_dangerous_memes.html.

89  Johnson, "The Meaning of the Zombie", my italics.

90  Liz Cole, "GreenCine I Zombies", [cited 13 November 2011]. Online: http://www.greencine.com/static/primers/zombies1.jsp.

91  Jamie Russell, *Book of the Dead: The Complete History of Zombie Movies* (FAB Press, 2005), p 171.

92  "Latest News—Battlefield LIVE Pembrokeshire", [cited 13 November 2011]. Online: http://www.battlefieldlivepembrokeshire. co.uk/news.shtml.

93  "Why We're Obsessed with the Apocalypse", [cited 13 November 2011]. Online: http://www.cracked.com/blog/why-were-obsessed-with-apocalypse/.

94  "5 Reasons You Secretly Want a Zombie Apocalypse", [cited 13 November 2011]. Online: http://www.cracked.com/article/136_5-reasons-you-secretly-want-zombie-apocalypse/?wa_user1=1&wa_user2=Weird+World&wa_user3=article&wa_user4=recommended.

95  R.C. Sproul, *Willing to Believe: The Controversy Over Free Will* (Baker Books, 2002), p 145.

96  Martin Luther, *A Treatise on Good Works* (this edition The Floating Press, 2009), p 91.

97  Sproul, p 145.

## The Japanese Domestic Toilet

98  Rose George, *The Big Necessity: Adventures in the World of Human Waste* (Portobello Books, 2008), p 53.

99  Washlet is the name for products of this sort made by the TOTO company. Chun quotes in-house figures that the Washlet alone constituted 32% of "home sales" of "sit toilets", and 38% of all "sit toilet" sales in Japan in 1997. Allen Chun, "Flushing in the Future: the Supermodern Japanese Toilet in a Changing Domestic Culture", *Postcolonial Studies* 5 (2002), p 159.

100 Chun, p 158.

101 Previously women would continuously flush the toilets to mask these noises, and "Sound Princess" was developed to save water. Santosh M. Avvannavar and Monto Mani, "A Conceptual Model of People's Approach to Sanitation", *Science of The Total Environment*, Volume 390, Issue 1 (2008), p 9.

102 George, p 59.

103 Julie L. Horan, *The Porcelain God: A Social History of the Toilet* (Robson Books, 1996), p 137.

104 Richard Craze, *Feng Shui: A Complete Guide* (Hodder & Stoughton, 1997), p 4, 17-18.

105 Arne Kalland, "Houses, People and Good Fortune: Geomancy and Vernacular Architecture in Japan", *World Views: Environment, Culture, Religion*, Volume 3, Number 1 (1999), p 46-47.

106 Kalland, p 35, 40.

107 Mary Douglas, *Purity and Danger: An Analysis of Concepts of Pollution and Taboo* (London: Routledge, 2002), p 50.

108 Patrick McElligott, Lecture on Japanese Religions at Oak Hill

College, 5th April 2008.

109 Horan, p 137.

110 Chun, p 154.

111 Including Alan Macfarlane, in *Japan Through the Looking Glass* (Profile Books, 2007), p 218.

112 George, p 51.

113 Peter N. Lundell, "Behind Japan's Resistant Web: Understanding the Problem of Nihonkyo", *Missiology*, 23/4 (1995), p 410.

114 McElligott, Japanese Religions, 2008.

115 Macfarlane, p 147.

116 Richard Keyes, "The Idol Factory" in *No god but God: breaking with the idols of our age*, Ed. Os Guinness and John Seel (Moody, 1992), p 45.

# ACKNOWLEDGEMENTS

This book has emerged from material I've been teaching at Oak Hill College and then out and about over the last fourteen years. Teaching and learning within the context of a residential Christian community remains a wonderful joy and privilege. So to Oakhillers past and present, a huge thank you.

Special thanks to Anja Lijcklama à Nijeholt, Martyn Beardsley, James Crooke and Rosanne Jones for graciously allowing their Oak Hill assignments to be used as worked examples. I take great pride in showing off your work.

Thanks to Carl Laferton at The Good Book Company for getting the project going and then his patience when it didn't. Thanks to my editor Rachel Jones for her skilful red pen (ok, "tracked changes") that has gently shown me that what I deemed to be "accessible" actually wasn't.

Thanks to Noah for reading an early draft, along with the rest of the Strange family subculture that continues to form me for the better: Elly, Isaac, Micah, Hetty, Keturah, Ezra, Gideon and Grandma.

Soli Deo Gloria

**BIBLICAL | RELEVANT | ACCESSIBLE**

At The Good Book Company, we are dedicated to helping Christians and local churches grow. We believe that God's growth process always starts with hearing clearly what he has said to us through his timeless word—the Bible.

Ever since we opened our doors in 1991, we have been striving to produce Bible-based resources that bring glory to God. We have grown to become an international provider of user-friendly resources to the Christian community, with believers of all backgrounds and denominations using our books, Bible studies, devotionals, evangelistic resources, and DVD-based courses.

We want to equip ordinary Christians to live for Christ day by day, and churches to grow in their knowledge of God, their love for one another, and the effectiveness of their outreach.

Call us for a discussion of your needs or visit one of our local websites for more information on the resources and services we provide.

Your friends at The Good Book Company

thegoodbook.com | thegoodbook.co.uk
thegoodbook.com.au | thegoodbook.co.nz
thegoodbook.co.in